Modern Bengali Poetry

Desire for Fire

PARTHIAN

BEE

Arunava Sinha translates classic, modern and contemporary Bengali fiction, non-fiction and poetry from India and Bangladesh into English. Fifty-one of his translations have been published so far. He lives and works in New Delhi.

Acknowledgments

Desire for Fire, an anthology of Modern Bengali Poetry in translation is one of the results of the The Valley, The City, The Village Literature Project which ran in 2018 involving a collaboration between writers from Wales and Bengal.

The publishers would like to thank all involved in the project and for the support of The British Council, The Kolkata Book Fair, Wales Arts International and Literature Wales.

The writers taking part from Wales were Natalie Ann Holborow, Siôn Tomos Owen, Gary Raymond and Sophie McKeand.

And from Bengal, Aniesha Brahma, Srijato Bandyopadhyay and Arunava Sinha.

A full colour celebratory magazine, *The Valley, The City, The Village*, featuring contributions from all the writers, is available from Parthian.

Modern Bengali Poetry

Desire for Fire

Selected and translated by
Arunava Sinha

PARTHIAN

Parthian, Cardigan SA43 1ED
www.parthianbooks.com
BEE Books
First published in 2020
© 2020 The contributors
Translated by Arunava Sinha
ISBN 978-1-912681-22-8
Editor: Carly Holmes
Cover Design by www.theundercard.co.uk
Cover painting by: Shipra Bhattacharya, Kokata
Image Courtesy: Sanchit Art, Agra/ Delhi
Photograph by: Rajesh Goenka, Kolkata
Typeset by Elaine Sharples
Printed by 4edge

Contents

Translator's overture

How many voices can a translator speak in? This is not a question that any translator has the luxury of asking. For they must be capable of having at least as many voices as the number of writers whose works they translate. And since each writer may speak in more than one voice, that means a translator's portfolio has to be even more versatile.

What usually works in the translator's favour, though, is that it's usually one voice per book. Of course, the challenge of harmonising with the original without going out of tune remains, but at least it is one band, or one orchestra, whose melody has to be followed.

The operative word here is 'usually'. This book is far from being usual in that sense, for it contains the works of fifty-four different poets, their poetry separated in time by more than a hundred years, which means a confounding variety in tone, idiom, vocabulary, sensibilities, technique, music, rhythm, and every other element of a poem.

In sharp contrast to this large cast of characters, there is only one translator. Is it possible for this one person to take on the personas of fifty-four others within the covers of the same book? Wouldn't it be far too audacious to make that claim? The answer is obvious.

As the translator, I ask you, the reader, to make a leap of imagination. Consider this book something like a concert, in which a musician sings cover versions of their favourite songs, whose originals were written and performed over a vast span of time. You will hear – or read – a great deal of those originals, of course, but you will also find the singer's own style a constant presence. Subtly, to be sure, and not at a volume or pitch that overshadows everything else, but still insistent, elusive and yet recognisable. As with any concert, the choice of what you will hear/read is entirely personal. This is the perfect moment to dissociate this selection from any attempt to represent a canon or to suggest that these are the 'best' works of modern Bengali poetry. The brilliance of the compositions are all thanks to the original poets. The false notes, if any, are the translator-performer's alone.

A first-timer's guide to modern Bengali poetry, aka The Introduction

By Ayan Chatterjee

Perhaps the most discussed, critiqued and controversial appellation in the history of Bengali poetry is 'modern'. There has been a diversity of views about modern Bengali poetry and modernity in Bengali poetry since the 1930s. It's superfluous to mention that the two forces of pre-Tagore Bengali poetry, Bharatchandra and Michael Madhusudan Dutt, were several steps ahead of their times. Therefore, if the word 'modern' were to be used to mean anything ahead of its times, these two poets would lead the list of modern Bengali poets. In reality, though, almost every critic from Buddhadeva Bose to Abu Sayeed Ayub were referring to the poetry of a particular period, of a particular kind, when they used the term 'modern Bengali poetry'. Specifically, it was the period between the two world wars – the 1920s and 1930s – and could be termed anti-Tagore or, at least, trying to break free of the influence of Tagore.

Rabindranath Tagore the poet transcends time. It is futile to look for the relevance of his poetry within a particular period or socioeconomic framework. The universality of his literature is the hallmark of his creativity. He was romantic by nature, and spiritual and joyous in his consciousness – a true devotee of beauty. Which was why, even amidst the invasions, treachery and procession of death that was the First World War, his sagely eye perceived the pleasure of the sunrise yet to arrive. Tagore was unique. To expect the same vision from others would be unrealistic. Even if the eternal perfection of time remained untouched in the poet's mental landscape, the world was burning at the time. The chronotope was changing rapidly. Meanwhile, the poetic aspirations of several mediocre poets were being dimmed under the radiance of Tagore's genius. In this situation, they were trying to follow and to imitate him to survive, with the result that an orbit of a certain class of poets was being formed around him. They came to be known as the poets of the Tagore school. Despite making a mark with one or two poems, none of them made an impact with their entire body of work. Among their ranks were Kalidas Roy, Karunabidhan Bandyopadhyay, Jatindramohan Bagchi, Debendranath Sen, Kirandhan Chattopadhyay, and Kumud Ranjan Mullick. Their work reflected none of the characteristics of modern Bengali poetry.

Freedom from Tagore's influence had now become an imperative for two reasons: to express the sensibilities of a period in which circumstances had changed, and to establish an independent existence as a poet. This endeavour became partially successful in the 1930s. But even before that, there were four poets in whose work a different note was heard for the first time: Mohitlal Majumdar, Jatindranath Sengupta, Satyendranath Dutta, and Kazi Nazrul Islam. They could be said to be a bridge connecting Tagore with the modern poets of the 1930s. Some critics would like to add a fifth name, that of Premendra Mitra.

In *Adhunik Bangla Kabya Porichoy* (*An Introduction to Modern Bengali Poetry*), critic Dipti Tripathi describes twelve characteristics of modern Bengali poetry, both in terms of sensibility and technique. Some of them are:

— Fatigue and despair under the assault of an urban, mechanical civilisation.
— Self-conflict and rootlessness.
— A conscious integration of diverse international cultures and traditions, such as Freudian psychology, modern physics, and Marxist philosophy.
— A deliberate rebellion against the Tagorean tradition and the search for a new path.
— The mixture of poetic and conversational idioms.
— Demolishing the classic form with random excerpts from eastern and western epics and the poetry or ideas of legendary poets, or bringing about a confluence between older traditions and newer sensitivities.
— Combining verbs drawn from everyday language with adjectives and adverbs drawn from Sanskrit.
— Copious use of apparent contradictions, irony, and remembrance – in other words, of metaphor.

Needless to state, not all of these qualities are to be found in the work of a single poet. But the most important poets whose works display the majority of these features are Buddhadeva Bose, Jibanananda Das, Sudhindranath Dutta, Bishnu Day, and Amiya Chakraborty. Theirs are the most prominent names among the poets of the 1930s – that is to say, of the early period of modern Bengali poetry.

~

Modern Bengali poetry was born primarily in the page of a single magazine from the first half of the twentieth century.

Its name was *Kallol* (1923). While older poets like Mohitlal Majumdar and Nazrul Islam were published here, so were a number of newer poets, including Jibanananda Das, Buddhadeva Bose, Amiya Chakraborty, and Achintya Kumar Sengupta. This new poetry made further advances through several other magazines published after Kallol, such as *Kalikolom* (1926), *Progoti*, published by Buddhadeva Bose and Ajit Dutta (1927), *Porichoy*, edited by Sudhindranath Dutta (1931), *Purbasha*, edited by Sanjoy Bhattacharya (1932), and, of course, *Kobita*, edited by Buddhadeva Bose (1935). Critics like Dipti Tripathi and Abu Syed Abu have identified the 1930s as the decade in which modern Bengali poetry was born, and there is no reason to disagree. Several of the most representative poets of this form were published and read at this time. The poet considered the finest in the Bengali language after Tagore was, of course, Jibanananda Das.

~

The 1940s were primarily a decade of political poetry in Bengali. Practically all the the poets who began writing in this period were followers of a leftist ideology, and their creations reflected this. Among the prominent poets who emerged were Arun Mitra, Jyotirindra Maitra, Dinesh Das, Samar Sen, Subhash Mukhopadhyay, Manindra Roy, Mangalacharan Chattopadhay, Birendra Chattopadhyay, Nirendranath Chakraborty, Ram Basu, and Sukanta Bhattacharya. If Bengali poetry sought to find a path for itself in the 1930s by rebelling against the Tagore way, the poetry of the 1940s can be described as a presentation of contemporary socioeconomic decay and a new political ideal. It must not be forgotten that leftist thought had not been able to establish itself as strongly in the 1930s as it did a decade later. Nor did the poets of the

1930s submit themselves to any particular political philosophy. But because the group of young poets who came into their own in the 1940s were deeply imbued in socialism, the themes of oppression, suffering, and deprivation quite naturally surfaced in their works. Their poetry also became more easily 'comprehensible' than those of their predecessors, for they took on the responsibility to reach out to the oppressed and deprived classes.

~

The 1950s also saw fresh changes in Bengali poetry, as in the previous two decades. The poetry written in this time falls primarily into two categories. On the one hand, older poets like Buddhadeva Bose, Jibanananda Das, Bishnu Day, Subhash Mukhopadhyay and Nirendranath Chakraborty were still in full flow, and could be considered established poets of the era. On the other, yet another wave of young poets was emerging though the pages of magazines like *Shatabhisha* (1951) and *Krittibash* (1953). Many of them were to be strong presences in the landscape of Bengali poetry over the next few decades. The names worth mentioning among them: Aalok Sarkar, Sarat Kumar Mukhopadhyay, Shankha Ghosh, Shakti Chattopadhyay, Alok Ranjan Dasgupta, Sunil Gangopadhyay, Tarapada Roy, and Utpal Kumar Basu. Any discussion of the poetry of the 1950s would thus have to include poets from both these categories. Of course, this is applicable to the subsequent decades as well.

The socioeconomic and political situation in India in general and Bengal in particular was precarious in the 1940s, halfway through came the violent pangs of the birth of two independent nations – India and Pakistan – and the Partition riots that led to the deaths, mutilation, rapes, and physical as well as psychological displacement of millions. By the 1950s, however, there was an attempt at consolidation. Just like nature's craving for tranquillity after a storm, so too did the themes of Bengali poetry in this period seek a certain calmness. The country had become independent only a few years earlier, in 1947. Everything was being cast afresh under a new Indian leadership. But the agony of the Partition – which saw massive migration and violence in Bengal and Punjab – was still being felt both overtly and covertly. However, the fires of the 1940s had largely gone out. Perhaps it was natural that the eternal themes of poetry would resurface in the works of those who began writing in this period. Love and nature, for instance, returned as the subject of poetry repeatedly. The impact of politics in general and leftist politics in particular was not palpable. This, however, was applicable only to those who began writing in the 1950s. Their predecessors, well-established poets by now, did not abandon their earlier concerns.

~

The poets of the 1960s can be divided into three groups. The first were those who began their journey in the 1950s, and were maturing now as poets. All the poets mentioned as emerging talents in the 1950s remained important figures in the 1960s. The second group comprised even older poets, who had started earlier and were still writing in their own unique ways, such as Buddhadeva Bose, Subhash Mukhopadhyay, and Nirendranath Chakraborty. The third group were the young poets who began their journey in this decade. The special features of the poetry of the 1960s really refer to the works of this generation. Among them were Bhaskar Chakrabarti, Kabita Sinha, Pabitra Mukhopadhyay, Saroj

Dutta, Samir Roychowdhury, Moloy Roychowdhury, Shaileshwar Ghosh, Debarati Mitra, Buddhadeb Dasgupta, and Manjush Dasgupta. Bengali poetry flowed in two primary directions in the 1960s. On the one hand was the significance of the Hungry Generation, which took the issue of obscenity in modern Bengali poetry all the way to the courts. On the other were three important sociopolitical developments which influenced Bengal's political landscape strongly. These were the 1962 war between China and India, which provided the backdrop for a bifurcation of views within the Communist Party, leading to its split in 1964; the food movement in 1967; and the Naxalbari revolution at the end of the decade. All three made a powerful impact on Bengali poetry in the 1960s (and afterwards).

~

The 1970s were one of the most momentous and controversial decade in the socioeconomic and political history of not just Bengal but all of India after independence. The Naxal movement lead to enormous social and political changes in Bengal. The Liberation War in East Pakistan, leading to the formation of the independent country of Bangladesh, and the Emergency in India – when fundamental rights were suspended for twenty-one months – were the two other significant events in this decade. Much of the poetry in this period centred around the Naxal revolution and the Liberation War of Bangladesh. Among the poets who emerged in the 1970s were Nabarun Bhattacharya, Joy Goswami, Mridul Dasgupta, Subodh Sarkar, and Brata Chakraborty. Not even the 'apolitical', self-reflexive poets of the Krittibash school of the 1950s and 1960s could turn away from the Naxal movement and the birth of Bangladesh. Shakti

Chattopadhyay had no choice but to write: 'It was not a very joyous time, not a very happy time.' Among the poets from East Pakistan-turned-Bangladesh, the Liberation War as well as the disappointment and despair of unmet expectations after independence appear as themes.

Two stars of modern Bengali poetry appeared in the 1970s. Nabarun Bhattacharya and Joy Goswami. Besides the fact of writing at the same time, they had nothing in common. In fact, they occupied opposite poles. Influenced strongly by a specific political ideology, Nabarun Bhattacharya considered writing poetry not just a literary pursuit but a part of one's social responsibility. Joy Goswami, on the other hand, was introspective from the very beginning. In the poems of the first of Bhattacharya's works published in this decade, *This Valley Of Death Is Not My Land*, we saw images of state-organised terror and blood-soaked descriptions of the sport of slaughtering the young. Questions rose in at least some people's minds over whether these killing fields indeed constituted their country. Meanwhile, Goswami was absorbed in the devoted pursuit of the eternal in his collection of sonnets of the winter and Christmas. In subsequent decades, too, he went on to bear aloft the legacies of Jibanananda Das and Shakti Chattopadhyay, rising to the status of being known as Bengal's finest poet in the post-Shakti Chattopadhyay era. The signs of these were evident in two of his collections, *A Set Of Christmas and Winter Sonnets* (1977) and *Ancient Creature* (1978).

~

If the 1970s spoke of the revolution, the 1980s were the period when the phoenix was reborn from the ashes. An entire generation, perhaps the most promisingly talented generation, had been wiped out by the Naxal movement and the violent response to it from the state. The 1980s became the decade in which new dreams were built on those ruins. Among the poets who rose to prominence in this period were Joydeb Basu, Rahul Purakayastha, Sanjukta Bandyopadhyay, Chaitali Chattopadhyay, Bithi Chattopadhyay and Mallika Sengupta. Besides these newcomers, those from earlier times who continued at their creative best included Shakti Chattopadhyay, Sunil Gangopadhyay and Joy Goswami. The poetry of the 1980s marked a departure from that of the previous decades. The political element used to be a powerful one in modern Bengali poetry until this time, with leftist ideas contributing a major part. But once the Left Front came to power in Bengal in 1977, the leftist poets were no longer anti-establishment. This was true of both the 1980s and the 1990s. Perhaps it was because the leftists chose the path of revisionism to incorporate themselves into the so-called 'bourgeois parliamentary democracy' that the revolutionary pen of leftist political poets began to lose its bite for the first time.

Although we still got the works of leftist poets like Joydeb Basu or Mallika Sengupta in this decade, somewhere their fieriness was beginning to fade by virtue of no longer being situated at the opposite pole to political power. And so political poetry could no longer continue with the tradition of being one of the most significant forms of modern Bengali poetry. The mainstream shifted to follow in Shakti Chattopadhyay's footsteps, with Goswami being the primary exponent.

In the post-Tagore area, a unique school of love poems sprang up in Bengali literature, taking the lead from Jibanananda Das. A chronological list of the students of this school would reveal four names in particular; Binoy Majumdar, Shakti Chattopadhyay, Utpal Kumar Bose, and

Joy Goswami. Significantly, all of them besides Goswami began writing in the 1950s, and of those three, two were members of the Krittibash group, Binoy Majumdar being the exception. Goswami entered the world of Bengali poetry a couple of decades after the other three, which made him the newest of the poets who followed the strains of Jibanananda Das's music when writing love poems in Bengali.

~

In the 1990s we came across an entire flock of young poets, such as Bibhas Roychowdhury, Yashodhara Roychowdhury, Pinaki Thakur, Sweta Chakraborty, Mandakranta Sen, Srijato, Binayak Bandyopadhyay, Suman Chattopadhyay, Sibashish Mukherjee, and several others. Another new feature of Bengali poetry became evident in this decade. All this while, every poet had ardently tried to create and nurture an original and unique mode of poetry for themselves. But in the 1990s this desire for individuality was crystallised into a collective consciousness. Barring a handful of poets, everyone's work began to display a certain congruence in form and language, a tendency that continues today.

Signs of the emergence of certain circles of poets became obvious as a result, the most powerful among these being the circle of poets affiliated to the Bengali literary and cultural magazine *Desh*. This was not the first time that the trajectory of Bengali poetry had orbited around specific magazines, one of which, *Kallol*, was closely associated with the very birth, as it were, of modern Bengali poetry. In the 1950s, magazines such as *Shatabhisha* or *Krittibash* were fellow-travellers on the road of change for Bengali poetry. So, in itself this was not an unprecedented phenomenon. Besides, *Desh* was neither a magazine devoted to poetry, nor a product of the 1990s, having been publishing the works of renowned as well as unknown poets for decades.

However, in the past, even if a group of poets associated with a particular magazine had grown popular, its members did not write their poetry in the same kind of form and language. In the first decade of the twentieth century, however, the similarities in the works of different poets became rather obvious, and this was a feature imported from the 1990s. Critics may point to the similarity between this and the works of poets in the 1920s, inspired by Tagore. But the two are far from being manifestations of the same forces. For one thing, the works of the poets of the 1920s resembled one another because they were all imitating the same poet. In this case, however, there was no one poet whose work was being mirrored. For another, there was a considerable difference in the quality of the respective poets of these two periods.

~

One of the most significant acts to take place in the 1990s in India was the advent of economic liberalisation, authored by Manmohan Singh under the leadership of PV Narasimha Rao, which changed the socioeconomic map of the country with a single stroke. The all-consuming philosophy of globalisation entered through the door opened by this policy, its mask of cultural homogeneity actually concealing the face of cultural appropriation. That its influence on modern Bengali poetry is deepening is evident, most of all, from the close juxtaposition of the body and soul in the poetry written by the circle of Desh poets. It is worth mentioning in this context that critics of leftist thought argue that it compares apples with pears, but the fact that capitalism, which stands at the opposite end from communism, does not do anything different is proven by the homogeneity that globalisation engenders.

Of the two principal Bengali poets of the 1990s, one, Joy Goswami, made his appearance in the 1970s. The other was not formally considered a poet, being known as a singer, lyricist and composer – Suman Chattopadhyay, who currently goes by the name of Suman Kabir. His lyrics could well be considered a form of poetry, with their publication in multiple volumes reinforcing the supposition. These examples of lyric poetry highlight Suman Kabir's prowess as a poet alongside his abilities as a songwriter, with some lines jumping out of the songs to become slogans in their own right. Borrowing images, situations and emotions from everyday life, he, along with Nachiketa Chakraborty, provided alternatives to the orthodox 'moon-star-flower-bird' tropes of poetry. He had the courage to capture the flow of nondescript, even mundane incidents, instead of relying on love alone, in his lyrics and poetry.

Shakti Chattopadhyay died in 1995 after reigning over the kingdom of Bengali poetry for as many as five decades. It was in that same decade, the 1990s, that his successor was identified in the form of Joy Goswami, who published most of his works in the same period, with nine volumes of poetry and what is arguably his most creative work, the 1998 verse novel *Jara Brishite Bhijechhilo* (*Those Who Were Soaked in the Rain*).

~

As we journey towards the final years of the second decade of the twenty-first century, we can see that the framework of Bengali poetry is changing continuously. Going beyond Srijato, the poet who rose to fame towards the end of the 1990s, Bengali poetry has found itself through the works of poets like

Rehan Kaushik, Raka Dasgupta, Samrajni Bandyopadhyay, Aditi Basu Ray, Aitreyee Sarkar, Abhimanyu Mahato, and others. Facebook has emerged as an alternative platform to books and magazines as a medium for publishing poetry. Talented young poems are today emulating Srijato's signature couplets.

Meanwhile, from the 1970s onwards, modern Bengali poetry in Bangladesh has proceeded on its own trajectory, with the liberation war and nature being constant themes for the first few decades, fused with an idiom that went from classical to contemporary within the space of a few years. It forms a diptych, as it were, with the oeuvre of poets from India.

It could be argued that the constant change in the landscape of Bengali poetry signifies the very flow of life. Its rapid evolution over the decades establishes the fact that time is indeed the fourth dimension of Bengali poetry. Which is why we can only end with a line from the ever-modern Tagore, 'I lose you every moment so that I may find you afresh.'

Translated from the Bengali by Arunava Sinha

Rabindranath Tagore

The greatest genius of Bengali as well as Indian literature.
Poet, lyric-writer, composer, novelist, playwright, short story
writer, essayist, philosopher, educationist, travel-writer,
Nobel Laureate.

Camellia

Kamala was her name
I saw it on the cover of her book
She was on the tram, going to college with her brother
I was on the seat behind hers
The perfect line of her profile was visible
Tender wisps of hair straying on her shoulder
In her lap were her books and notes
I didn't get off where I should have.

Since then I've been timing my departure
Though it doesn't match my working hours
Frequently it coincides with their hour of travel
Frequently I get to see her.
I tell myself, what if there's nothing between us
She's a fellow-passenger at least.
A pure intelligence
Seems to shine through her appearance
The hair swept back from her young forehead
Her bright eyes fearless.
I wished a crisis would erupt right now
I could fulfil my existence by rescuing her —
An assault of some sort on the road
A lout who was being impertinent…
It happened all the time these days.
But my luck was like a shallow, murky pool,
Incapable of holding anything historic
Ordinary days croaked drearily like frogs
Sharks and alligators weren't invited, nor swans.
One day there was a crowd, some jostling

A half-Englishman was seated next to Kamala.
Without provocation, I was dying to knock his hat off,
And throw him out by the scruff of his neck.
I couldn't find a pretext, my fingers itched.
At that moment he lit a fat cigar
And began to puff on it.
Going up to him, I said, 'Throw it away.'
Pretending not to hear,
He blew smoke-rings deliberately in the air.
Plucking it from his mouth I tossed it out.
Balling his fists he glared at me —
Then leapt off the tram without another word.
He probably knew who I am.
I was well known as a footballer,
A bit of a loud reputation.
Her face turned red,
Opening her book, she pretended to read.
Her hands trembled,
She didn't even glance at the hero.
The office clerks said, 'Good for you.'
Soon afterwards she got off, before her destination,
Took a taxi and went on her way.

I didn't see her the next day
Nor the day after.
On the third day I spotted her
Going to college on a rickshaw.
I realised my bull-headed error
She was quite capable of looking after herself
I needn't have intervened at all.
I told myself again,
My luck's like a shallow, murky pool —
The memory of my heroism echoed in my mind

3

Like a mocking bullfrog.
I decided to make amends.

I'd heard they usually vacationed in Darjeeling
I needed a holiday urgently that year.
They had a tiny home, it was named Motia —
In a corner down a slope from the road
Behind a tree,
Facing the snow peaks.
I was told they weren't coming this time.
Contemplating return, I ran into a fan
Mohonlal —
A little sickly, tall and bespectacled,
His weak constitution perked up only in Darjeeling.
He said, 'My sister Tanuka
Won't let you go without meeting you.'
The girl was like a shadow
Her physical existence the barest minimum —
Not as keen on her meals as she was on books.
And hence such unusual admiration for a football captain
She thought it generous of me to meet her.
What games destiny plays!

Two days before my return to the plains, Tanuka said,
'I'll give you something to remember us by —
A flowering plant.'
Such a nuisance. I was silent.
Tanuka said, 'A rare, expensive plant,
Needs a lot of care to survive on our soil.'
'What's it called?' I asked.
'Camellia,' she answered.
I was startled
Another name flashed in the darkness of my mind.

4

I smiled. 'Camellia.
Its heart isn't to be won easily, is it?'
I don't know what Tanuka made of this,
She was embarrassed suddenly, pleased too.
I set off, along with the potted plant.
It turned out she wasn't an easy co-passenger.
In a carriage with two compartments
I hid the pot in the bathroom.
Never mind the details of the journey,
Forget, too, the triteness of the months that followed.

The curtain rose on the farce during the autumn vacation
In an area where tribal people lived
A tiny village. I'd rather not reveal its name —
Compulsive holiday-makers aren't aware of its existence.
Kamala's uncle was a railway engineer
He had set up home here
In the shade of a sal wood in squirrel country.
Where the blue mountains could be seen on the horizon,
A stream coursed across a bed of sand nearby,
Silkworm were cocooned amidst the flame of the forest
Oxen wandered about beneath the trees
Unclothed tribal boys perched on their backs
There were no houses to stay in
So I pitched my tent by the river
I had no companion
Only the camellia in its pot.

Kamala was here with her mother.
Before the sun was overhead
While the dew-soaked breeze blew
She strolled in the sal wood with her parasol.
The wild flowers bowed in prayer at her feet

She didn't even spare them a glance.
Crossing the stream with its thin trickle of water
She went to the other bank,
To read beneath a tree.
That she had recognised me was obvious
From the fact that she didn't notice me.

One day I saw them picnicking on the sandbank.
I had the urge to ask, don't you need me for anything.
I can fetch water from the stream —
Chop wood and bring it from the forest,
Besides, isn't it possible to find
A decent bear in the jungle nearby?

I spotted a young man in the group
In shorts and an imported silk shirt
Sitting beside Kamala with outstretched legs
Smoking a Havana cigar.
While Kamala absently shredded
The petals of a white hibiscus
An English monthly magazine
Lying by her side.

In this desolate corner, I realised,
I was unbearably redundant, I wouldn't fit.
I would have left immediately, but for an unfinished task.
The camellia would bloom in a few days
Only after sending it to her would I be free.
I roamed the jungle all day with my gun
Returning at dusk to water the plant
And check on the progress of the bud.

It was time, finally.
I had sent for the tribal girl
Who brought me firewood every day.
I would send it with her
In a leafy box.
I was reading a detective story in my tent
When a melodious voice wafted in, 'You called for me?'
Emerging from the tent, I saw
The camellia tucked behind her ear
Lighting up her dark-skinned face
'Why did you call for me?' she asked again.
'Just for this,' I replied.
And then I travelled back to Calcutta.

An Unexpected Meeting

We met suddenly on a train
I hadn't thought it possible.

I'd seen her over and over
In a red sari
Crimson like a dahlia;
Today she was in black silk,
It covered her head in a cowl
Cupped her face, lustrous and fair like a lily.
She seemed to have enveloped herself
In a deep dark distance,
The distance to the edge of the mustard-fields
To the blue-grey of the sal wood.
My senses came to a sudden stop,
I knew her once, now she wore a stranger's solemnity

Throwing aside her newspaper
She greeted me suddenly
Social mores could now be followed;
We began to converse—
'How are you?', 'How is everyone?'
Etcetera.
She continued to gaze out of the window
As though she had overcome the contagion of intimacy
She answered in monosyllables,
Some, she didn't even respond to.
Conveyed with an impatient wave—
Why talk of all this,
Silence is so much better.

I was on another bench with her companions.
After a while she beckoned with her finger.
Such boldness, I thought—
I sat down on the same bench.
Under the sound of the train
She said softly,
'Please don't mind,
Where's the time to waste time!
I have to get off at the next station;
You're going further,
We'll never meet again.
So, I want your answer to the question
That hasn't been answered all this time,
You'll tell the truth, won't you?'
'I will,' I said.
Still gazing at the sky outside she asked,
'Are those days of ours that are gone
Gone forever—
Is nothing of them left?'

I was silent for a while;
Then I said,
'All the stars of the night
Remain under the glare of the day.'

I felt doubtful, had I made it all up.
'Never mind, go sit over there now.'
Everyone got off at the next station.
I journeyed alone.

Nazrul Islam

Resplendent in his own glory even under the dazzling sun of Tagore. His celebrations of love and revolution earned this poet-lyricist-composer the title of 'the rebel poet'.

The Song of the Students

We are the power and the force
We are students, all
Tempests die beneath our feet
Cyclones spiral overhead
We are students, all

We defy obstacles by night
We travel barefoot
Even this hard ground flows with blood
Beneath our iron steps
In every generation our
Blood has soaked the earth
We are students, all

All our lives are out of control
Streaking meteorites
We are the constant sacrifice
For the gods of fate
While goddess Lakshmi visits heaven
We enter the blue seas
We are students, all

Yes, we hold the horse's reins
The king of death rides on
It is our deaths that write
The history of our lives
To the land of smiles we bring
Tears of destruction
We are students, all

While the rest are clever and wise
We make all the errors
The cautious build dams everywhere
We just flood the banks
On dreadful nights we make the streets
Slippery with blood
We are students, all

Our eyes blaze like knowledge beams
Our hearts are full of words
The clarion calls of eternity
Are ringing in our throats
With fresh blood we have reddened
Saraswati's white lotus
We are students, all

When the revolution comes
We will lay down our lives
Within us weeps liberation
Of the centuries
We have all shed tears of glory
To fill our mothers' hearts
We are students, all

We are writing the future
Of love and of hope
The Milky Way points us towards
The road to paradise
Let the people of the world
Keep dreaming through our eyes
We are students, all

Jibanananda Das

The finest Bengali poet to follow Tagore. His best-known volumes of poetry are *Bonolota Sen* and *Ruposhi Bangla* (*Beautiful Bengal*). Enjoys cult status. Died in a tram accident.

Bonolata Sen

A thousand years, and yet I walk these paths
On darkest nights from Ceylon to Malay seas
I have wandered; Bimbisar and Ashoka's grey lands
I was there; further still, in Vidharbha's dark cities
Life foams around my weary soul again
She brought me a spell of peace – Natore's Bonolata Sen

Her hair as dark as Vidisha's ancient nights
Her face sculpted in Sravasti. Like the lost sailor
On the distant ocean, the ship's rudder broken,
Who sees a green land in a cinnamon isle
In the dark I've seen her. 'What kept you?' she asks, and then
Raises her bird's-nest eyes – Natore's Bonolata Sen

Like the sound of falling dew at end of day
Evening comes; the hawk wipes the sun-smell off its wings;
The colours of the world fade, and the manuscript
Twinkles in firefly hues for all these tales
All birds come home – all streams. All transactions end
Only darkness remains. And – face to face – Bonolata Sen

If we were

If I were a wild swan
And you, one too
By the river on a horizon
Near the ricefield
Within slender shafts
In a secluded nest

Then on this spring night
Gazing at the moonrise behind the casuarina rows
Leaving the smell of the water in the lowland behind
We'd let ourselves float over the silver harvest in the sky
My feathers in your wings, the pulse of your blood in mine
Millions of stars like golden cornflower in the indigo sky

In the shaggy green siris forest
Like an egg of gold
The spring moon
Perhaps a gunshot
Our oblique momentum
In our wings, the euphoria of pistons
In our throats, the song of the north wind

Perhaps a gunshot again
Silence for us
Peace for us
No more of the fragmented death of our life
No splintered thwarted wishes and darkness
If I were a wild swan
And you, one too
By the river on a horizon
Near the ricefield

A strange darkness

A strange darkness has descended on earth
The blind have the clearest vision today
The world stops moving without the advice
Of hearts that beat with no compassion or love
Those who still trust deeply in humanity
Those to whom the great truths and traditions
Or art and learning still appear natural —
Their hearts are food for jackals and vultures today

Amiya Chakravarty

Arguably the most outstanding among the modern poets of what came to be known as the 'Kallol Jug' ('A New Wave'). His poetry is marked by a sharp and oblique idiom.

The Exchange

In return you have got
The silent pool in entirety
A clear mirror framed in blue
Water filled with light
A shadow branch that's bent with flowers
Fluttering sails of purple clouds
Filling up the heart
An empty breast finds all it seeks
In return you have got
Blanked out thoughts of nothing-at-all
Open roads for feet-with-dust
Bereft-of-tears, the wind
A distant cry, a familiar voice,
This afternoon of all-is-lost
No-glance-back from anyone
Are these what you've left

On the Island of Santa Maria

Antony lies beneath the moist green church field

[Villager 1]
'Do you have some comfort at last?
Does the memorial stone with your name above feel heavy?
Can you still hear the whispering willow deep underneath?
Antony, they say in the depths you have found your
    heavenly home.'

[Villager 2]
'If you walked up here you'd find your vision unbound
The old village road, the river you know in the south
Where home was, by bluish waves in the cornfield
If you took a bus to the market, ready to travel afar,
Where Fernandes, your neighbour, sells Coca-Cola.'

[Widowed sister]
'Antony, we cannot hear what you say any more
Still I wish for your laughing banter, your gentle face
Shy and distant, gazing in rapt attention at your work
You look for something – drawing your glasses to yourself
As before. Somewhere, though, the exchanges have stopped.'

[Foreigner, passer-by, friend]
'Leaving paltry physical senses to the five elements
You seek, I think, the deeper touch of soul; here the world
Swells, placing you in burial and prayers on the far side
Of grief and tears, evening chants rise quivering in the air
Do you hear Antony, Antony, in the solemn notes of bells?'

[Friend's wife]
'Your child left first, you lie by her side, beneath
Your gravestone, the third, empty place is Margarita's,
She is here every day, bowing to accept the weight
Of remembrance of husband and child, who knows what
     hope
Puts a shimmering glow of silent prayer on her face?'

(The church bell peals incessantly)

[Chorus]
'We have not forgotten, Antony, even if we leave the church
     for home now,
We will leave for our final home too – only, some earlier,
     and some later.'

1604 University Drive

Not behind me, but together. Rippling
Hair touched by a wild wind, casuarinas rustling,
The aroma of coffee, the butter on the toast tastes of honey
The cool maddening pink light at seven-thirty in the morning
This momentary materialisation
Gathered in physical sensation
Mixed with the fragrance of eau-de-cologne
I'm sending you distant wings at the edge of the blue
The chugging of the train, the stilled sunlight at the station
A sinking feeling from last night's dream
Arriving and yet looking back
There's the bell to start teaching my class, a busy breeze
My house is in Lawrence, where the golden grain ends
On the stairs the hour of saying goodbye pauses
(The address is still the same, sixteen-oh-four)
Here's my gift with the embedded memory of cologne

Sleepless Woman

I know you're not sunk in slumber
So I lie down secretly in the thick of night
To tell you, listen,
On this bed beneath a roof of the sun and stars
  — the night a fine mesh strung across it —
How long the day stretched for us
Breathing in separation – at last I touch you like a shadow
How strange we two are to us
Sleepless woman
Suddenly the moonlight falls on the white bed
I find you're gone

Premendra Mitra

Poet and writer of mainstream as well as genre fiction. Multifaceted talent who also wrote scripts and directed films. Trendsetter among modern Bengali poets.

My city

My city isn't all that very old
Bones or coins or convents from the past
Will never be found buried in its soil
From traders' boats moored at the bank
It had stepped ashore with muddied feet
Just the other day, amidst coconuts and palms
Just the other day, and yet, so long ago
So much dew has dropped on it since then
The heat has baked it so many times
Its feet are soiled by so much dust and grime
So much smoke and soot have blurred its sight
My city has entirely forgotten
The primordial rhythm of its life

Still, when days for shedding leaves arrive
And sudden gusts of wind now and then
Ruffle the crowns of trees above the roofs
For a while my city is then roused
From its drowsy sleep

With chimney stacks staring at the sky
Who knows what it ponders over then
Does it get the meaning of its life?
It's put up bridges, set up mills
Built markets full of shops
Laid out shows of colours on the roads
But still there is a wild and ancient swamp
Lying beneath the surface of its heart

Words

Even afterwards there are things to say
After it has rained
Like the soil-smeared smell of a wet cool wind,
Blurred, like clouds
Who knows whether they're words
Or a trembling vibrant silence

I shall not say these things to her
In pauses between the determination and effort to survive
My astonished heart
Tells itself in solitude
All these mist-like words
I have whispered many strange things
How much of what the heart means
Can these words hold anyway

Like snow all these words melt
On a lofty peak
Of passion
I touch a hand with my hand
Grope within my heart with words
Do we have each other still?

And so when all my words
Have been defeated, a sigh
Flows, and perhaps indifferent time
Trembles inadvertently, once

And then in every crack of existence
The fog settles, and words
Like the fog, roll towards the horizon

Buddhadeva Bose

Extraordinarily talented, this teacher, poet, novelist, translator, critic and editor was not only a pioneer of modern Bengali poetry, but he also brought Jibanananda Das's poetry to readers. Founder of the comparative literature department at Jadavpur University.

Bloomington, Indiana

How quiet this Sunday morning is – the streets deserted,
    the houses
Asleep behind curtains, rows of unemployed cars. In this
    country
No one gets out of bed before one o'clock on Sundays; the
    roads
Lie like canvases with the silence of the trees on either
Side.

But when I went out I heard a tring-tring sound behind me.
Tring, tring, tring. A few minutes' gap, and then again.
Again. Again. Wounding the tender body of the wind
The sound rose – piercing, voluble, ardent –
I walked along and, following me, this sound seemed
Unending.

What message was the telephone ringing with – in whose
    house,
For which hero, which friend, which lover? Was it someone
    in distress
Waiting on the other side?
Had someone's loneliness proved unbearable?
Had death visited someone? Or was it some mute sorrow,
Some unspoken grief that finally wanted to be heard like a
Bugle in this incessant ringing of the telephone bell?

But could no one besides me hear it?
Was I the only one awake on this street? Citizens,
Wake up. Hero, friend, lover, hold out your arms
Awaken, heart. Awaken, agony. Awaken, consciousness.
    Listen

27

To the cries, 'Save me, save me!' They are for you
Only for you, this announcement – these are those same tears
That keep flowing across the world like an unceasing current

In a secret melody, they materialised for you today, this
    moment,
Spreading out in one wave after another. Someone wants you.
You are needed – you, the fortunate one.

I don't know when the sound stopped, don't know whether
    someone
Sank into despair, all I know is that the one who calls out
Is vulnerable, the one who expects is helpless – for sometimes
The telephone rings in numbed rooms, some letters never
Reach, and the language of what must be said is inaccessible.

Meanwhile the June sky was bright, the wind once again
Calm and invigorating, the leaves rose and fell like breath
And the houses were stilled as usual behind curtains of
    sleep.

Chilka Morning

How wonderful it felt this morning, today—
How do I tell you?
How pristine blue this sky, so unbearably beautiful
Like unfettered, unbound notes from a singer's throat
Flowing from horizon to horizon
How wonderful it felt to gaze at this sky
Wavy lines of green hills all around, misty with fog
And flashing in their middle, Chilka.

You came close, sat for a minute, then went off that way
For a look at the train that had arrived at the station.
The train left. How I love you—
How do I tell you?

The sun has flooded the sky, impossible to look at
The cows are tearing at the grass intently, so quiet.
Did you ever imagine we would find here beside this lagoon
What we had not found all this time?

The silver water lies in bed, dreaming; the entire sky
Cascades on its breast in a torrent of blue
At the kiss of the sun. An exquisite rainbow will blaze
Around the ocean of your blood and mine—
Did you ever imagine this?

Yesterday we saw from our boat on Chilka
A pair of butterflies winging towards us from the distance
Over the water. Such audacity! You laughed, and
How wonderful it felt.

Your beautiful, shining face. Look
How blue this sky is and how many skies
Are trembling in your eyes, how many deaths, how many
     new births—

How do I tell you?

The Burden of Responsibility

Nothing is easy, nothing is easy anymore.
Writing, reading, checking proofs, letters, conversations,
All that distracts, for now, from the quotidian burden—
Everything. Like a giant forest, a devious alternative
Appears, argumentative like a mountain of shrewdness.
Defeated every time in that battle, having died,
When the heart said, living only with the body
Is most preferable and wanted, for nothing else
Is serene, soothing, unwaveringly affectionate—
When I, thinking it faithful, submitted the essence
Of my self to the embrace of a dazzling lover—
And watched from a distance, although that generous rescue
Obliterated thought, reading, conversations,
Envying love and the lover, a cruel dowry ushered in
The burden of a difficult, newer, unforgiving responsibility.
Nothing is easy, nothing is easy anymore.

Manik Bandyopadhyay

A writer who believed in Marxist philosophy. Primarily a novelist and short story writer.

Tea

We bribe London to drink our tea

The gardens are on our mountain slopes
Our workers plant the seeds
It's our labourers who pick the leaves
They're naked, uncivilised, black-skinned.
As black as burnt charcoal.
Drinking the tea he makes, the white king says,
What a perfect cup of tea.
Advertisements with smiling faces announce
The world's finest nation, England's
Ritual of tea at four.
How fierce these advertisements
Like the furtive pride of a foreign addict
Turning tea into a catalytic agent
For ensuring a chemical reaction between a woman
And a man drinking tea out of a tin mug
Because they both sip tea, they
Are equals
Connected.
The society lady with seductively silken trembling hands
Pours tea into the cups of the Lords
The labourer drinks his tea on the street
Without a serving of biscuits
Cold, watery tea with no milk or sugar.
Who knows?
Whose blood is this tea?
The extract of whose life, youth, hopes, joys?
Whose sterile desire to give birth?
The pain of which whippings in jail?

Whose agony of being raped as virgins?
The poison from the churning of whose lives?
Who wants to know all this as they drink their tea!
They drink their tea too
In clay cups on the roadside
Those whom tea has turned pale and ashen
The eggs and meat of red-faced Whites
Their milk and their cream

And humans they eat to treat deserved diseases

Fresh blood is reddish
Oozing out of the dead, it's blackish
So isn't the extract of tea
A watery syrup of blackish blood?
Isn't it the nectar in a crystal goblet
Mixed with soda and sugarcane juice?

We're wild beasts, intent on protecting meat and gore
In a mad frenzy for blood!
A beautiful cup and saucer, the glint of flintstones
Polished to a gentle glow

The hidden inscription beneath, Made in England.
To save England, with generous American style
We dedicate our lives to sipping tea in china cups.
We bribe London to drink our tea.

Young Girl

Dark young girl, white sari, what style!
Rebelling against being passed over by beauty.
In her eyes a brimming desire for the moon and the harvest
Beneath the marquee the critics of her dark skin are gathered
The fair wife, fair daughter, fair daughter-in-law
In glittering jewellery and gaudy clothes
Dying of envy, alas.
Just look at that girl
You're dark, your eyes have no play of kohl
No densely set coiffure for your hair
On your lips no subtle touch of a lipstick
Your blouse is ignorant of the glory of your breasts
You have no folds in your skin anywhere.
A dark-skinned girl are you
The way you dress it doesn't seem
You're a girl.
You're a revolutionary who's left home
You're a rebel
Who knows, maybe you're even a Communist.

Bishnu Dey

One of the most important poets of the early period of modern Bengali poetry. Renowned for using epics and for reusing Tagore's poetry in his own.

Bauhinias

Where are those days now? Their memories
Only awaken in my loneliness
The other's a hero in the war of life
Where's the glory in loving remembrances?

Patchwork repair on either side of time
Still let's one of us see an intense sky
That room, and by the window, bauhinias
On whose branches two people had grafted
A single opportunity.
                              Today
One of them no longer seeks the flowers
A gardener plants dahlias and zinnias
In pots on the staircase, and a servant
Brings the blossoms into the chamber.

The bauhinia sheds its petals by my room.

Dinesh Das

Socialist poet of the 1940s. His most famous poem, 'The Sickle', earned him the epithet of Kaasté Kobi, or Sickle Poet.

Hone that Sickle My Friend

Bayonets might be pointed
Hone that sickle, my friend
Shells and bombs may pack a punch
Is the sickle sharp, my friend?

Did the young crescent moon
Make you fall in love?
It's not the century of the moon
The sickle is the moon above

Those who had filled the world
With cannons and with lead
Have been ground to dust today
By cannon fire instead

So this world of leaden dust
Melts in your blood-sea of red
Turning into clay and earth
The age of land lies ahead

Gathering on the horizon
There's the earth my friend
Is your sickle sharpened?
The sickle of land, my friend

Samar Sen

A prodigious talent, this journalist, editor and poet was a believer in socialist political ideologies. Founding editor of the journal *Frontier*.

An Unemployed Lover

Day after day I wander about in the thieves' market
In the morning at the tap
Fatigued prostitutes clamour for water
At night I hear ships at Kidderpore dock
Sometimes I have exhausted thoughts
I cannot sleep, god of love. I smoke
And on the city roads I watch with all my might
The soft, arrogant breasts of white women
And during bewitching midnights sometimes I say
Liberate me from this deathless love
Bring a new world to the planet
Hurl a day like an upraised steel blade
I wake up in the morning
To the tired hubbub at the tap
And my bloodstream burns throughout
In the arid desert of the trader's civilisation.

Urvashi

Will you flow into our middle-class blood
Like clouds racing across the horizon
Or will you flow into our dismal lives
Now that you are so tired, Urvashi?
Like the fertile women who flow into
Chittaranjan maternity home
With the hungry fatigue of unfulfilled nights
And many sighs
How many green mornings like bitter nights
How much longer

Subhash Mukhopadhyay

Made his entrance in the world of Bengali poetry like a
warrior with his poem 'Padatik' ('The Foot Soldier') in the
1940s. A socialist poet who changed the voice of his poetry
several times.

My Son's Gone into the Forest

~ 1 ~
So Ram went into the forest
His father Dasharath's
Heartfelt agony
Was wiped out in just six nights

How strange to think that, with this kind of common sense,
Balmiki made sense of seven acts for this harsh world
If I were to write
I wouldn't summon the blind sage without reason
To make destiny bend to my will

Talking of writing, I recall, once upon a time,
Longing to be a writer
I had the evil desire to pierce the target by its sound
(I was still in the throes of virginity)

Hé Ram, shame on me
Pardon this indiscretion on your servant's part, lord
Piercing the target by its sound…
That slipped out in mere carelessness

I am not an inadvertent murderer who fired an arrow at the
    sound of water
I have not been cursed
By a grief-stricken blind sage

I don't expose my tear-stained heart and summon people to
    view it
I am not subjugated by my wife

A doubt-stricken, nerve-shattered, effete Ikshvaku king
In silent pride I bear the punishment of time.

Now that the hour has come for me to go into exile,
My son has gone into the forest
Leaving me bonded
Still I am a traveller; in my hand the drums of war are
    thudding

Come closer, Ratnakar, go away, Balmiki.

~ 2 ~
Beads of sweat on my brow
Time stands still
Like a tram immobilised
By a snapped overhead cable

To wage a war for freedom
My son has gone into the forest
Leaving me bonded

A man at the next table
Is coiled like a snake
I'm keeping a strict eye on the soda bottle
I shall not go over the limit
I'll seek the company of old memories
Shaking off all my anxiety

Even if I don't get a train
I'll push a paper boat along
Carry my shoes and walk home

I shall shed dewdrops from the fields along the way
Let the river overflow its banks
And threaten me with its high waves
I want again the wonder I felt as a child
The thrill of walking in the dark with a lantern

My son has gone into the forest
Leaving me bonded

Although they knew they wouldn't find him
Policemen came in two vans late last night
Scouring the house with their guns cocked
Trying to rake up a fire that's almost dying
After forty

My son has gone into the forest
Leaving me bonded

And yet it is in his hands that I see unfurled
Coronated as prince
My own pennant

Let flowers bloom or not

Let flowers bloom or not
It's spring
On the paved footpath
Its feet dipped in stone, a coarse and hardy tree
Its ribs bursting through tender leaves
Is laughing
Let flowers bloom – or not
It's spring.
Putting a blindfold on the eyes of light
Before removing it,
Laying down a man in the arms of death
Before taking him away,
The days that have passed along the road
Had better not return.
The little boy who could mimic
The cuckoo for a couple of coins,
On early evenings bathed in turmeric yellow
Just like a pre-wedding ritual
Has been called away by the days.
Over her head a sky like a
Yellowed letter written in red ink,
A dark ugly spinster from this lane
Had pressed her breasts against the railing
Pondering over all this.
At that moment
Defying what it could see, a damned bad-ass butterfly
Flew up to sit on her body, for heaven's sake!
Then the slamming of a door
Covering its face in the darkness
The gnarled tree
Was still laughing

A May Day Poem

This is no time to play with flowers, my love
We are face to face with destruction
Blue wine dreams are gone from our eyes
And skins baked by a searing sun
Listen to the chimney's bugle-siren
The hammer and sickle are singing
We die every moment but still we live
And we love the millions who are living
Give all obstacles the dowry of passion
Let your nails and teeth vow to kill
Aroused rhythms will snap all chains
Bright days lie beyond the hill
The weeping of the downtrodden century
Brings shame with every single breath
Put on the armour for battle now
No more waiting like cowards for death
This is no time to play with flowers, my love
The news of destruction is here
What if we lose our way in the storm?
To young souls the road will be clear

Birendra Chattopadhyay

Adherent of a specific mode of leftist political thought.
Began writing poetry in the 1940s.

Antiwar

Let us go to the land of the moon
Let us, while there's still time, fly our respective national flags
In the land of the moon, on its highest peak
Let us make its ground more valuable than gold

On earth there are no more rivers or hills or sky
Nowhere is there six feet of land to sleep beneath
Not even the meagre shelter of a bird's nest
Or the soil for a blade of grass to stand on
Today our past is the dream of history, a grandmother's
    fairytale

In vain do people seek the glow cast on their own faces
By the lustre of mutual hatred on television and journalists'
    panels
In vain are humans proud of their own country, their own
    party
In fact there are no signs of the existence of earth beneath
    their feet
Where six feet of land can be measured out for colonisation

Let us go to the land of the moon
If we can spare the time let us give it, dearer than gold, a
    national anthem
And then, when the moon is extinguished and the
    grandmother's chanting ends
We will make fresh calculations and suck up the land on
    Saturn and Jupiter and Mars
Like Agastya did, we are people who desire peace
We need six feet of land to survive

Niren, Your Naked Emperor

Niren! Your naked emperor
Has only changed his clothes
Or is it the king who's changed?

Where's that child today?
The one who spoke the other day
Can you tell us, Niren
Where he's gone?
Or won't you speak up any more
You got a pay hike today

Heigh ho, heigh ho
Without your clothes, Niren
You are naked too
But then whoever keeps
A mirror like that at home?

Not this emperor, nor that
Neither you not me
Heigh ho, heigh ho
Without our clothes, Niren
We are all naked

We are all emperors in our
Kingdom of kings
But you won't understand, for
You got a pay hike today

Flames Dance Between Flints

Flames dance between flints. Holding fire,
Men dance, look. Night dances, winter dances
Between flints – the cold mountain dances
The night mountain dances. Red, like flames
A thousand red flags dance, ending the night
In the eyes of prisoners. They dance, dreams dance.

Nirendranath Chakraborty

Socialist poet who started writing in the 1940s. The accessibility of his works have made him a widely-read poet.

The Naked Emperor

Everyone sees that the emperor is naked, but still
Everyone claps
Everyone cheers. Well done. Well done.
Some out of tradition, some out of fear
Some have pawned their brains to others
Some beg for food, some are
Favour-seekers, lobbyists, frauds
Some think royal robes are indeed so fine that
Even if invisible, they exist
Or, at least, it's not impossible that they do

Everyone knows the story
But in this tale
There weren't just some eulogy-mouthing
Complete cowards, tricksters or idiot
Flatterers
There was a child too
A truthful, forthright, courageous child

The emperor in the story is in the real world now
Again the applause is continuous
A crowd of flatterers
Has gathered
But nowhere in the mob today do I see
That child

Where has the child gone? Has someone
Hidden him in a
Secret mountain cave?
Or has he, playing with stones and grass and mud

Fallen asleep
By some
Desolate, distant river, or in the shade of a tree in the wild
Go, somehow or the other,
Find him
Let him appear before this naked emperor
And stand boldly
Let his voice be heard but once above this applause
Where are your clothes, emperor?

Jesus of Calcutta

There was no forbidding red light
But still Calcutta, rushing at breakneck speed,
Has stopped suddenly
Desperately regaining their balance
Taxis and cars, trucks, double-decker buses with tigers'
    faces
Those who ran up screaming from both sides
Of the road
Porters, vendors, shopkeepers, customers
They too are frozen like images pinned on
The artist's easel
In silence everyone watches
A completely naked child
Crossing from one pavement to the opposite one
On tottering feet

It has rained just a while ago in Chowringhee
Like an extra-long spear, the sun has again
Pierced the heart of the clouds
To descend
Calcutta is bathed in a magical light

My face framed in the window of the state-owned bus
I look alternately at the sky and you
Child of a beggar mother
Jesus of Calcutta
You have stopped all traffic with your spell
The shrieking crowds, the grinding teeth of impatient
    drivers
You care for nothing

Death looms on either side, between them
You wobble forward
Like personified humanity, you want the entire world

In your hand
From the joy of learning to walk.
That's why With teetering steps, you
Are going from one corner of the universe to another

Inhuman

You were so very depressed today, chimpanzee
At the zoo. You were by the lake.
Sitting morosely. Not once did you
Climb on the iron swing-set made for you
All the bananas and peanuts and chickpeas
Were untouched. You didn't throw them a glance
Like a miserable man you sat there alone
Burying your face in your knees

Why were you so depressed today, chimpanzee?
What saddens you? To be just like a human being
You climbed a staircase stretching across
Millions of years, only because you missed the final steps
Did you not end up as human. Was this regret what kept
    you
Sitting unhappily by the lake?

You were so very downcast today, chimpanzee
You were almost there, but you didn't become
Human, perhaps it was this despair
That kept you away from the swings today
You did not perform tricks like a half-human
To please young and old, maybe you didn't notice
Or you did, that just like apes, the audience
Tittered at you and went off to the tiger's cage

Sukanta Bhattacharya

A believer in radical leftist thought, he began writing poetry in the 1940s but died when he was only twenty-one.

The Permit

The child born tonight
Brought me news
The release documents have arrived
And so she asserts her right
At the door of the new world
With a sharp cry
Her tiny body is defenceless
Still her fist is clenched
Upraised, glowing
With an inscrutable pledge
No one understands her tongue
Some laugh, some scold mildly
But in my head I have grasped the language
Received a letter from the age that is coming
I read the identity papers of the newborn
With clouded, foggy eyes. A new child
Has arrived, we must make room for her
On this decaying earth, a failure in ruins
We must leave – and we will
But still, as long as I live
With all my might I will clear the filth
I will make the world worth living
For this child
This is my vow to the newborn
Finally, when it is all done
With the blood in my veins I will bless
The child just born
And then become history

The Cock's Tale

A cock suddenly found shelter
In a small corner of a huge mansion
In a heap of broken packing boxes
With two or three more hens

Although there was sanctuary
There wasn't enough food
Protesting sharply, this cock
Simply went hoarse screaming
From dawn till dusk...
Durable and mammoth, the structure
Couldn't care less

Then he began visiting the garbage bin
Incredible! Every day there seemed to be
Plenty of delicious food – all thrown away

Then came others to stake their claim
Two or three people in dirty, tattered rags
So, being weaker, the cock got food no more

Food! Food! Some food!
Helplessly searching for food
The cock tried to storm the mansion
Being chased away every time.
The small cock dreamt, its head held high—
'Piles of food inside the mansion.'

Then one day he indeed got entry
Managing to go directly
To the banquet table draped in spotless linen;
Not to *have* food, though—
But *as* food.

Shubo Acharjya

Having begun writing poetry in the 1950s, he subsequently became part of the famous Hungryalist Movement.

The sounds of a dog
with no duties

Thrice I've exchanged glances with a dog with no duties
Noting at the base of every lamppost on the street
A distinctive self-contradiction, I advance, it can also
Be called retreating there's no fear of being ambushed
All movements are unrestrained and using the alphabet,
Words like 'love' and 'death' are utilised for sport
Every day on the beach, just this instant I have put
A hand prone to criminal acts in my empty pocket
With the other I tickle the featureless chin
Of the world, saying, 'dance little lady dance' —

Manindra Gupta

A progressive poet, once a believer in leftist ideology.

The Collection

It began with stamps—
Then matchboxes, coins, masks, butterflies, pebbles,
And finally meteor fragments.
But all this is suitable only for children—
After this, soon after, I had my eye on adult male objects.
And I can say, my proud collection now includes
About fifty chastity belts used by European virgins,
Parts of a native American warrior's scalp, complete with
    ponytail
And tufts of hair, scraped off while he was still alive,
Murderous axes of headhunters from Nagaland and Borneo
Saris used as nooses by suicidal Bengali women (two of
    them silk)
Tattooed skin from the back and stomach of Maori beauties,
Post-holocaust black yellow and white foetuses at various
    stages.

At present I am looking for
The brain of a sage in a trance, and
A round peg that can fit perfectly in a square hole
Or vice-versa.

Sarat Kumar Mukhopadhyay

One of the people behind the legendary poetry magazine *Krittibash*, he began writing in the 1950s.

Side by Side in Two Rooms

They live in two rented rooms, side-by-side
There's just the one bathroom, though,
And one kitchen. But nothing else is shared.
Sometimes this one says,
I'm too tired to cook
Will you add a little rice to your pot for me?
Another day the second one says,
I'm exhausted
Let's play a game of chess in your room
On all other days, mostly
They do not even meet
Work remains busy with work
Pleasure, with pleasure

The pet dog

Observe the pet dog closely.
Harassed, fed up by imprisonment at home
Constantly straining at the leash, as though
Wild animals are calling him to the jungle

He hasn't received military training, still
When he scents a stranger
With a roar he launches himself at the door
As though he would tear the intruder apart if only he could.

Observe the pet dog closely.
Resting his head like a ripe papaya
On his front paws he's wondering
Was my acting credible today?
I hope I'll get my dinner tonight.

Lanterns

I heard the man was something of a daredevil once
His education ended in Class Nine
For thrashing the headmaster
I heard he has travelled the entire world
As a deckhand
He was in Latin America for ten years. Apparently
He speaks fluent Spanish.

And his wife: her face is like a glass lantern now —
It seems legions of men used to pursue her.
I heard she had at that time
Tried to hang herself from the ceiling
Those who knew why are no longer living

From the seventh floor room to the seventh floor room in
    that building
Parallel
Neither of us bothers with curtains at that height
I see the man dusting cobwebs off the walls sometimes
Sitting with his legs splayed, polishing his shows
The soles of his feet are swollen like loaves of bread.
His wife tastes the food as she cooks it
Or lies in silence on the bed.

Only, at four in the afternoon
Exactly at four, by the clock, every single day
They sit opposite each other. They drink tea.
Two smallish heads, swollen faces.
Very high above the street
Two extinguished lanterns.

Kabita Sinha

One of Bengal's foremost post-independence feminist poets and writers.

I keep coming back
to be humiliated

You call me repeatedly to be humiliated
I keep coming back
I have a need for humiliation.

You call me with a mirage clasped in your hand
Your lips talk of friendship – prosperity
I have a need for humiliation

You call me repeatedly to be humiliated
I keep coming back
In a court of high-pitched jesters
Naturally the sari runs out
You see
I have no supply of cotton

You call me repeatedly to be humiliated
I keep coming back
Unlocking the cages, you let loose the dogs of disgrace
I have a need for disgrace.

There's no need to change your battleplan
So don't hold out
Your hand to shake mine
There's no silken smoothness to my palms

Shankha Ghosh

This poet and academician, who began writing in the 1950s, has carved out a unique space with his spare, intellectual poetic style.

Advertisements hide my face

All alone I wait for you
In the lane I find my place
I think of giving you a glimpse
But advertisements hide my face

I think I'll signal with my eyes
A simple truth or maybe two
They glitter in the gaudiness
Of advertisements coloured blue

It's hard to tell how one man sees
The other one – with love or scorn?
But oh my exaggerations
But oh the land where I was born

Once my eyes were locked with yours
But now my glances have been sold
The neon creates commodities
Of private stories never told

All the things I meant to say
Are in that lane now, languishing
But my mask, so exhausted,
Dangles from the advertising

Babar's Prayer

Here I kneel towards the west now
Spring has arrived empty-handed today
Destroy me if your will so desires
Let my descendants remain in my dreams.
Where has his transparent youth vanished
Where does decay gnaw away furtively
Abject defeat in the corner of my eye
Pours poison in my arteries, lungs and veins.
Let the azaan from a grey emptiness
Awaken the extremities of the city
Turn me to stone, make me quiet, still
Let my descendants remain in my dreams.
Or is there no relief for the future
In the germs of sin that my body bears?
In celebrating my own barbaric win
I summon death to my own house.
Or do the flashing lights in the palace
Burn all my bones, even my heart,
And allow a million foolish moths
To find a home deep within my frame?
You have endowed me with many things
Where will you put me when I'm in ruins
It's better that you destroy me, oh god
Let my descendants remain in my dreams.

The Poet in Italy

The train is running from Florence to Turin
The year is 1926, the 18th of June
At Milan station a duke appears, saying softly
'What you see is not all there is. All I can say
Is that it's best not to talk politics.
Speech has no freedom here. And all these murders…'
Abruptly the train leaves. Creases on the poet's brow.
Has there been an indiscreet mistake, after all?

He seemed a worthy leader, energetic, devoted to the nation
He seemed an artist too, the kind seen in artists' eyes
All true. Then why does Benedetto Croce slink home
     furtively at dawn?
Why is there suppressed fear on so many people's faces?

After Turin the poet visits Rolland at Villeneuve
His friends silent, Rolland wonders: Is it possible?
From him we want to hear of liberated thought
Of the independence of reason in our work
Can he be so blind?
The poet must broadcast how the historian Salvemini lives
     abroad
Why, for that matter, the exiled Salvadori languishes in
     Zurich
The gash of protest splitting whose face is woven in blood
Terror and tyranny across the country behind closed doors
He must explain that this is a time of existence
When the leader crawls in public before the lumpen's raised
     finger
That this is a time when

Decibels alone can turn blatant lies to immaculate truth
This is a time when
In a lawless land the only law is the dictator's wish

This is a time when
Killers consign innocent flesh to sacrificial flames in every
    home
You have not seen all this, poet
You have only seen a festive, cheering, resplendent,
    bejewelled Rome

Rolland was silent, silent his aggrieved friends
Listeners frowned. He must have made a mistake then
He had to tell the world of his change of vision
With pain and shame the poet took his pen up again

Drunk

Make him a little more drunk
How else will he
Bear this world easily.
He's still young, lord!
Age him now, then—
How else will this
World bear him easily.

Shakti Chattopadhyay

The finest Bengali poet in the post-Jibanananda Das period, he added a new dimension the rhythms of Bengali poetry. He earned a reputation for a reckless, Bohemian lifestyle.

Postmen in the Autumnal Forest

I have seen postmen wandering in the autumnal forest
Their yellow sacks filled with grass like swollen sheep
    bellies
So many letters new and old they had found
Those postmen in the autumnal forest
I have seen them pecking away incessantly
Like a solitary crane at a fish
So impossibly, mysteriously, warily absorbed
They're not like those postmen of ours
From whose hands our constant, indulgent love letters
Are lost all the time

We are moving away from one another continuously
Distancing ourselves out of greed for letters
We are getting many letters from far away
We are going away from you at once to hand over letters
Loaded with love to the postmen

And so we are moving away from the kind of people
We are ourselves
And so we are about to express our foolish weaknesses
And motives, everything
We can no longer see ourselves in the mirror
We keep floating in the unpopulated evening veranda
And so we are taking off our clothes to be swept away
Alone in the moonlight
For a long time we have not embraced one another
For a long time we have not savoured human kisses
For a long time we have not heard people sing
For a long time we have not seen babbling children

We are drifting towards a forest even more ancient than the
    forest
Where the mark of eternal leaves is fused in stone jaws
We are floating away to a land of such unearthly connections
I have seen postmen wandering in the autumnal forest
Their yellow sacks filled with grass like swollen sheep bellies
So many letters new and old they had found
Those postmen in the autumnal forest
The distance between letters has only grown
I have never seen the distance between trees grow

Not a very happy time

Tottering from head to toe, from wall to wall, from parapet
    to parapet, swapping pavements at midnight
On the way home, a home in a home, feet in feet
Breast in breast
Nothing more – (a lot more?) – even earlier
Tottering from head to toe, from wall to wall, from parapet
    to parapet, swapping pavements at midnight
On the way home, a home in a home, feet in feet, breast in
    breast
Nothing more.
'Hands up' – raise them high – till someone picks you up
Another black van in a black van, and yet another
A row of windows, doors, a graveyard – skeletons lying
    awry
White termite in the bones, life in the termite, death in life –
    therefore
Death in death
Nothing more.
'Hands up' – raise them high – till someone picks you up
Throws you out of the van, but into another one
Where someone waits all the time – clutching plaster like a
    banyan seed
Someone or the other, whom you don't know
Waits behind the trees like a hardy bud
Holding a golden cobweb noose, he will
Garland you – your wedding will be at midnight, when
    pavements are swapped, tottering from head to toe
From wall to wall, from parapet to parapet
Imagine the train waiting while the station runs, starlight
    by the dying bulbs

Imagine the shoes walking while the feet are still – heaven
and hell turned upside down
Imagine children trotting to the crematorium bearing the
corpse – in afterlife
Decrepit men dancing horizontally at a wedding

Not a very happy time, not a very joyous time
That's when
Tottering from head to toe, from wall to wall, from parapet
to parapet, swapping pavements at midnight
On the way home, a home in a home, feet in feet, breast in
breast
Nothing more.

The Rain on Calcutta's Breast

We hadn't asked for it, still the rain, like galloping hooves
Rang out on the tin shed, flowers were sprinkled on the road
A stain trickled down the garbage hillock, a different
Black torrent facing ugly houses instead of bungalows
Of Calcutta, the rain came, the rain flooded the bylanes
Swept away stories, rags, fish scales and peel, everything
The humidity in middle-class homes, insurance policies on
Strewn scraps of paper, voting ballots, dry wood shavings—
All of these. From the rain to the picnic in the rain, all of it
Is useful for Calcutta, dead grass – that's useful too
The labour room on one side, crematorium ashes on the other
Birth and death, all the details, are neatly arrayed in the rain
In a satin case inevitable lumps of cottonwool rest
The rain goes to bed a little late on Calcutta's breast

The Girl Named Mungri

With many rocks it has covered the path
The tiny stream that flows past the heart
Across it, houses by a linseed farm
If only you had known the girl named Mungri
You'd like it if you knew how the breeze
Suddenly makes her bunched-up hair fly
Whispering rain, with the flowers dropping
Pollen, the distant mountain-woods of teak
It's not building a home in another's mind
Nor opening the moon's doors and windows
The tiny stream that flows past the heart
Across it, houses by a linseed farm
If only you had known the girl named Mungri

Purnendu Pattrea

A multifaceted talent, this poet and artist directed films too.

From 'Conversations'

Not today, but for a long time now, Calcutta's phones
Have sworn not to allow anything but dirges to be heard
But this sudden call?
How'd you get my number?
Who told you this is the hour
When I'm alone in my cave?
Where are you calling from?
Greece or maybe from Paris?
You haven't been in Calcutta for seven years
Are you back?
When?
Speak a little louder please
When it comes to intimate conversations
The telephone is not just an obstacle or fence
It's bruising barbed wire
You startled me when you called out my name
Subhankar? He's a lie
A figment of imagination
Non-existent on this sunlit earth
Privately created by someone, he's just
A personal plant
Is it you, then?
Really you?
I didn't, to tell the truth, imagine this
The flute of spring in the glare of summer
Is beyond my dreams
~

Getting hold of your number?
That's a long story.
Ten times I scoured that thick directory

Couldn't find your name anywhere
Want to know how I got it at last?
I met Shyamal suddenly at Nandan
At the Chaplin festival
He parted with the precious information
How long have I been back?
Nearly three months
In a gondola in Venice, at Pompidou Centre in Paris
On Mozart or Chopin nights at the Barbican in London
While swimming waterless in a speedboat on a Swiss lake
At the Vatican, the heaven of Sistine Chapel in my eyes
And at all those other places when I lived in Europe
I thought of you, and then
The flame went out, or I
Snuffed it out myself
But as soon as I was in Calcutta
The dead fire was reborn
All my feminine principles were shattered
The moment I saw the softly overcast Calcutta skies
The knee-deep water on Calcutta's pavements, submerged
    carts,
Within me, the rain
A devastating dance of clouds, lightning, storms
Calcutta's trees are dressed in your clothes
Your passion is on the Metro Rail
The neon lights are your dazzling eyes
You're all over Calcutta
You are Calcutta
What time are we meeting?
When? And where?
At the Cannes Festival I learnt
From your former devoted journalist Subrata
That you've given up cigarettes for a pipe

I've got you other presents too
Picasso, Matisse, Modigliani, Braque, Paul Klee
Magnificent, marvellous prints
An ashtray from Florence painted like Michelangelo
Anything more you'll get
Is open to guesswork
When? Tomorrow? In the evening?
Where? What? Hello?
Hello, speak louder, hello
I can't hear a thing, hello, hello
My god!

Miracles

That's how miracles happen
Suddenly an ordinary seashell cracks open
Blinding white moonlight flashes inside

You rolled like a pearl into my palm
The scene changed at once
To my right was a cloudy day
It turned into a split pomegranate sunshine
And on my left the pile of bricks
Arranged itself into a red-tiled cottage

That's how miracles happen

Memory is So Wayward

An old pocket yields a dried rose from who knows when
How old is it? Who gave it to me? Was it in spring or in
winter?
The corpse of the rose holds no remembrance to be
deciphered
Do I have memories, for that matter? Are they organised
Like bookshelves or long-playing records and cassettes
The way songs and conversations are integrated and
catalogued?
Memory is so wayward, as though it's a violent gust of
wind
Delighted with hide-and-seek, smash-and-grab, topsy-turvy
Even on melancholy afternoons it sings, can sing, joyous
notes
Wings of desire have merged with clouds and vapour in the
sky
Fiery days have melted into the green of newborn grass
Dearest faces have dissolved in the blue within the ocean
Memory is so wayward, recalling everything even after two
millennia
Like the hunter it knows well the form and murmur of the
forest
Yet it won't say who gave me the rose yesterday or the day
before

Sunil Gangopadhyay

Founder-editor of the legendary literary journal *Krittibash*, and one of the most important poets of the 1950s and beyond. A novelist and short-story writer as well as a poet, his life too was converted into an urban legend.

For Neera, Unexpectedly

Three minutes at the bus-stop, yet for hours in my dream
    last night
I saw you embedded like a knife across the ocean—
    compass-less—
One body like the fifty-two holy places, in the wind
I saw you last night in my dream, Neera, in the dire blue
    times
Of dreams that ripen once and die.

When did you visit the southern sea-door, with whom?
Have you only just returned?
How terrible, how silent the ocean was in the dream,
    without a wave,
As though it would kill itself three days later, your horizon
    in the distance
Like a lost ring, your knees immersed in the blue water
Suddenly you seemed to be a gambler's moll
And yet you were alone, alone in the intense dream.

I shan't sleep for a year, wiping the sweat off the brow
At dawn after a dream seems so very foolish
I prefer forgetfulness, as free of shame as
The naked body hidden in clothes, I
Shan't sleep for a year, for a year I'll be awake, dreamless
And roam your body, like the fifty-two holy places,
To earn my piety.

Your smiling face in the bus window, 'I have to go,
Come home sometime.'
The shriek of the sunlight drowns all sounds.

'Stay a little longer,' or 'Let's go to the library garden.'
Someone

In my heart said these things, glancing at my watch with
Remembering eyes I jump up, leapfrogging over the road,
    buses, trams,
Carts and people
Loping on all four limbs like an orang-utan
I reach the door to the office lift.

Three minutes at the bus-stop, yet for hours in my dream
    last night.

Exile

Nikhilesh and I, that is, I and Nikhilesh, that is, the four of us
Together in the evening
Walk though Curzon Park – princess lights all around us
The insurance company's clock makes us fearful
As its hands run backwards, our figures have bent
Heads, the four of us walk by, cigarettes change places
On our lips, we don't talk, from the multihued flower
Gardens on either side of Red Road coloured winds blow,
    like
Magic with cards the cars come and go, what matches this
Is the breath of a dying river, we walk on, we had been to a
Broken-down factory to buy chains, we're returning, I
Look at the other three and they, at me, sidelong glances
In bright and dim lights our shadows are equidistant
Twisting my ankle in a rathole or wormhole on the moonlit
Field I drop back, they don't notice, they walk on
Sometimes they're in the light, sometimes in the shade
    beneath trees
They don't turn back, they don't stop, they go on…
I call out to my shadow in an atheist's voice, a hundred
    girls' screams,
Plus laughter, rise thrice next to the Memorial
Shielding it, this time I shout my name out very loud
Before anyone can answer, an auctioneer bangs his gavel, as I
Am about to throw a stone someone asks, 'Sunil, what
Are you doing here?' Wiping the blood on my knee and brow
On the grass I see at once trembling reds and greens in the
    dark
I want to raise my arms upwards to cover the jury of
The Great Bear, 'Get up, come home, or tell us

Where have you hidden Neera?' A man cannot be
    recognised from
His voice, a blind girl had once told me, instigating my eyes
I had investigated the man; who can walk down the path
    where
There's no sin, no sorrow? As though a hunter had arrived
    after
Traversing a dense forest, the sharpest question of life
On his lips, he stood, touching with fingers like temple
    spires
A blue emptiness – as though so familiar, yet the face is not,
Nor the eyes, so heartless the man had no shadow, a
    lifetime's sorrows
Rose in my breast, 'Where have you hidden her?' 'I don't
    know' The words
Like blood on the brow, but still they don't understand the
    language of blood
Thirst and failure keep asking, I don't know where I have
    hidden Neera, or
Where Neera has hidden me. Where was Nikhilesh lost, in
    existence
The shadow and the figure, each other... I kept walking
    alone again for a long time
No one came along – not the question, not the shadow, not
Nikhilesh, not love
Only exile

Got the Blues

Got the blues
Got the blues
Got the blues
No one knows
It's a secret
Not on my face
My eyes are open
Though they're closed
No one's noticed
Day after day
The days pass by
In hope, in hope
In hope in hope in hope in hope
And now my lips
Cannot taste
The tastes they love
Not even woman
Not even woman
Not even woman
Not even wine, not even words
Got the blues
Got the blues
Got the blues
At sundown
On my own
On the streets
On my own on the streets on the streets
Seeking nothing
Going nowhere
Wanting no one
Seeking nothing going nowhere

I'm a man too
All I have
Or all I had
All I have or all I had
In the flower
In the seed
In the worm
Like flames like flames like flames and flames
Got the blues
Got the blues
Got the blues
Still they pass
The days just pass
In hope in hope
In hope in hope in hope in hope

No One Kept Their Word

No one kept their word, thirty-three years have passed, no
    one has
In childhood a wandering minstrel had suddenly stopped
    and said
She would sing the rest of the song three nights before the
    full moon
So many dark nights have eaten up the moon since then but
    she
Never came.
For twenty-five years I've waited.

Nader Ali, the boatman at my grandfather's house, had
    said, grow up
I will take you to see the lake at Tinprahar
On a lotus you will see a snake and a bee
Playing
How much more do I have to grow up, Nader Ali? Must my
    head
Pierce the ceiling of this room and touch the sky before
You take me to see the lake at Tinprahar?

I never managed to buy a single Royal lozenge
The gloating Laskar boys would suck on their lollipops
Like a beggar I stood at the Chowdhurys' gate to peep at
The Rasa festivities
Amidst a constant stream of colour, fair-skinned women in
    golden bangles
Laughed in different pleasures
They never spared me a glance

My father had touched my shoulder, saying, one day we'll
    also…
He's blind now, we never got to see anything
No one will return to me
The Royal lozenges, the lollypops, the Rasa festivities
Tucking a scented hanky into her breast Baruna had said
The day you love me truly
My breast will also be just as fragrant
For love I took my life into my hands
Wrapped a red rag around a wild bull's eyes
Scoured the universe to bring back 108 blue lotuses
Still Baruna didn't keep her word, her breasts only smell of
    flesh now
She is still just any woman
No one kept their word, thirty-three years have passed, no
    one does

Binoy Majumdar

This rare talent of the 1950s was both a mathematician and a poet. His poetry is infused with mathematical philosophy.

Come back, Wheel: June 22, 1962

Then let it, let it all burn, the fountain, the gaping, wounded
    heart
Let peace stay away, let me forget all satisfaction
Let my body, my soul, fill with my agony for her
Her eyes, oval like a boat, had held the intense call
Of the ocean, shadows, clouds, rainstorms, the sky, the
    wind
Like the memory of the blossom that pricks with its thorn
Her thoughts won't go; this agony, it is as secret, as sweet
As the sting of the membrane torn at the first lovemaking
Then let it, let it all burn, the fountain, the gaping,
wounded heart

Soumitra Chatterjee

Best-known as an actor and theatre-person, but also a writer, poet and co-editor of the library journal *Ekhhon*. Inspired by leftist ideology.

New World Symphony

1

At the entrance to heaven
A tourism poster hangs
I stand beneath it
Holding immigration papers

No more music now
No more of counting the stars
In the circus of fairies and nymphs

The band plays
Many hippos, many giraffes
And a walrus
Moving in a queue
Towards the entrance to heaven

Beneath the tourism poster
I wonder, floating in my dream,
When I will wake up
And tell the boy at the tea shop
Can you wash the cup in warm water
And give me some tea

2

I'll see only the eyes
Of the man who's playing the violin
When he's done playing
He'll talk to a cat
Walking along the top of a wall
The cat will disappear
Then he will put the violin to bed

And say words of love
To a poem
I'll see only his eyes
Eyes in which October is blazing
The man who's playing the violin

3
The afternoon ended at this point
At the crossroads anguished by echoes

Before that
The summary of your figure
Touched my heart
In a very short time
And, like an echo
Vanished in vibrations

The afternoon ended at this anguished crossroads

Perhaps this is the best way to be
When the traffic lights turn green
From the anguished crossroads, two echoes
Vanished in their respective directions

4
A black man with a banjo
A Spaniard with a guitar
Listening to them
He climbs up to the concrete freeway
He can hear the drumbeats of the tyres
The blazing Texas sun overhead
He's come a long way in search of what doesn't burn even
    when burning

Spotting the sky, he says
Come, clouds, give us some shade

Black people's jazz
The white symphony of the New World
Take the exits from the freeway
One by one to spread out
Across the entire continent

Now he
Genuflects to Whitman's poetry
Come, poet, give us some shade
Tell us how
Amidst such storms and currents
We can frame a song

5
This mountain, this lake
Present a scene
That I will make sure to remember
And tell you of one day

I will make sure to remember
The melody in my flesh and blood
That rang out like a waterfall
The sigh from this expanse
That made a home in my heart
And take them for you

These streets, this stop sign
The architect's automobile dream
This Harlem, with memories
Of slaves male and female

This blue song of darkness I will remind you of
On an evening of yours

When one day I will
Present my love to you

6
I got very late saying goodbye to the sun
The crowds have thinned downtown
I used to call the one or two people
Sitting on roadside benches old men
They're my age now

I'm assuming
You once viewed my youth the same way you view
All those people racing along the sidewalks

It's time to return home after a long weekend
The moon came to a stop above the fiftieth floor
Rising from the bench
Floating into the air like a helium balloon
From my eyelids drooping with exhaustion
My slumber
Climbed upwards to touch the moon

7
Just a little further on, the river
Will have its speed limit raised
Automatic transmission will turn it into
Fast-flowing rapids
And then a giant waterfall

Then
Desiring a supple rainbow
It will leap into eternal uncertainty

Just a little further on, the river
Will forget itself
And turn into the sea

8
I can say it now
While the setting sun talks to me
I can take the wrong exit by mistake
Lose my way for a while
And then return to you
While the golden dusk talks to me

The Chhotonagpur plateau in the evening
Like this one, did you want to find a way there too
Here the stone highway took us such a long way
Still our eyes are worn out looking for hope
Yet it can be said right now I can say
While the setting sun talks to me

9
The man's gigantic
Black – or perhaps white – or brown
The man's very heavy
His shadow's even heavier
Shadows of sad people weight a lot more

In search of his television
The man is driving very fast
His dinner

He'll race out of the car
And sit on the couch facing the TV
A city will
Be lost then within a shadow
The shadow of a sad man

Out of the subway and into the streetcar
Shadows racing in search of their television
Saturday market on the waterfront
Young women shopping in young men's boutiques
Bright young women
Without any shadows

The shadow of a sad man
He's huge, black – or perhaps white – or brown
Very heavy
His shadow's even heavier

10
The forest approached
The deck behind the house
Drew up a chair

A pitch black squirrel will appear
Pluck and eat a pear from the tree
Run up and down the apple boughs
Signs of the slave age in the apple orchard
Does the black squirrel know them?

At times the sound of the traffic
Will waft from the road behind
To the deck
Chat with the forest
The whispers of the river will be audible

The day the barbecue will blaze
Tinkling sounds will come from the party
Unrestrained currents of laughter.

11
The day has been accounted for in creating dreams
After which a vagrant darkness
Is crowding my breast
Making it impossible to have those dreams
My road meanders
From one darkness into another
From one violence into another

The woman in the ghetto is drunk
In another life or another land
She could have been my wife
If I knew the armed mugger's name
He could have been someone like my son

Under the guise of abundance
Enough food is thrown away every day
To girdle the planet end to end
The scent of the food makes seagulls
Forget the coast and sky inland
And borrow babies' voices to weep

Dreaming of the New World
Strangers from everywhere arrive
Like those seagulls. Consigning
The old sanctuaries to the flames
And conducting their funerals, one day
They'll throttle their weeping till it dies
From the innards of one violence

I travel towards another one
As I make dreams, the wretched darkness
That closes in around my breast
Is not the dream I wanted to have
I travel great distances from one continent
To another continent with a dream of love
So that I can love you once
No, twice
No, a million billion times

Syed Shamsul Haq

A poet from Bangladesh, he was also a talented novelist and short-story writer, and hugely influential on subsequent generations of writers.

I will pause a moment

I will pause a moment and go away;
I will stop only a moment before I leave;
No, I didn't come here to stay;
This is not my destination;
I'll just pause for a moment
And then go away
From here.
I'll go away
Swiftly through this city of yours
I'll leave hurriedly
Beside the equation of march-pasts
Beneath the helicopter pacing up and down.
I'll go away
Under the constant vomit
Of the ticker-tape from
The windows of your commercial blocks.
I'll go away
Evading the unblinking eyes
Of the collection of bio-datas
Inside your computers,
Just the way I was going towards my destination
Slowly
Over a long period
Over one
Two
Three
Generations.

I promise
Not to kiss any of your women

I promise
Not to take any of your children in my arms
And I promise
Not to apply for any of your apartments
Not to accept loans from your banks
Not to join your administrative councils
Not to contest in your elections
And I also promise
Not to give speeches on your radios
Not to feed data into your computers
Not to demand rides in your helicopters
Not to beat the drums at your march-pasts
Your apartments cause me pain
Your ovens cause me pain
Your banks cause me pain
Your councils cause me pain
Your mirrors cause me pain
Your glasses cause me pain
Your women cause me pain
Your children cause me pain
I'll just pause a moment to observe
My way home passes through all of these
I'll go home
On the way to every home in the world
Are cities like these
I'll move on in a moment

The apartments you have, I know, have no roofs
The ovens you have, I know, have no fire
The banks you have, I know, have no wealth
The councils you have – achieve no consensus
The mirrors you have – throw no reflections
The glasses you have – hold no water to drink

I know
Your women cannot bear children
I'm aware
Your children have no seeds of grains in their hands

With several wars and a single peace
With several famines and a single harvest
With several silences and a single utterance
With several genocides and a single boat
With several flags and a single independence
For one two three generations
I have been moving on continuously
With the sensation of
A red throbbing of an ugly wound in my body
In the direction of a house that never collapses
In the direction of an oven that never goes out
In the direction of a bank that never goes bankrupt
In the direction of a council that never declares war
Towards a mirror with reflections
Towards a glass with pure water
Towards a woman who has just let her hair loose
Towards a child who has just drenched itself in the rain

This progress that I'm making
Is progress through all of you.

Ploughing through the nights like an alert beast
I continue beneath the moon in search of water,
Tearing through the silence like a spider's web
I move on like a man trapped in a cave
Led by the sound of water.
I still do not know whether what's waiting at the end
Is a woman or her beads unstrung from her necklace;

I still do not know whether what I'll see at the end
Will be the moon in a lake or skulls in the mud.
Still I must go
And still I simply must go, with a thousand wounds.
Passing through this city of yours
If I should glimpse a rare couple
Whose song the wind is still keen to bear,
I know I too wanted to be a couple
So this momentary pause.
If I should glimpse some torn scraps of paper,
In them imprisoned some poet's fragmented words,
I know that I too wielded a pen to write verses —
So this momentary pause.
If I should glimpse a white flower which bloomed
In the night with a brief but sharp fragrance,
I know that I too have dreamed in the garden —
So this momentary stopping.

Prepared for the night, a woman is calling me,
I must go;
With the possibility of poetry a sheet of paper is calling me,
I must go;
Rich with saplings, a garden is calling me,
I have no choice but to go;
A child is calling me
A nation is calling me
A mirror is calling me to stand in front of it.
So after a brief pause I'll go on
The way I was going
Slowly
Over a long period
Over one
Two

Three
Generations.

It is through all of you that my path has always run
And always I have paused only to continue on it.

Tarapada Roy

Starting out in the 1950s, this poet was associated with the Krittibash group. He was also a popular writer of *belles lettres*.

Testimony

I shall tell the truth, the whole truth
My lord, your honour
Your servant had no illicit relationship
With the deceased Shantilata
It is true that once I brought her
Lily seeds from Mourigram
Our family has no face to grow plants
Like lilies and grandiflora
My lord, your honour
It's hard to explain what I mean by no face
Simply put, one may say
It's forbidden to grow these plants
Anyway, I had hoped that our neighbour Shantilata
Would plant them in her garden at the back
And every morning I would feast my eyes
On the lilies through the southern window
Shantilata did just that.
I would feast my eyes regularly
There was no sin lurking unbeknownst
Occasionally I would see Shantilata too
My lord, your honour
There was nothing more sinful than this
Between her and me.

Pranabendu Dasgupta

The greatest asset of this poet from the 1950s is his accessibility, but that takes nothing away from the depth of his poetry.

The Ducks

Some people have released ducks in my life
That's why the sounds begin every morning, loud sounds
The clams and snails have remained, I think
Or else why all these ducks right now?
Had we ever imagined
That our water would be muddied this way
Who are the people who released all these ducks?

We finished much of our work before
Visiting the pond
It would have been better if the water were crystal clear now
Perhaps we would have swam, or sat here in silence
Speaking in low tones with the deep shadows

Who are the people who released all these ducks?

One Dead Bird

The bird lies dead
The bird lies dead within a pile of snow
Was it somewhere earlier? Had it built
Its nest in a blue tree on derelict land?
Or did it fly around on the pretext of a wind
And come to its camp in this second house to die.

It's buried its head beneath the snow
As though there's a room in there
It was supposed to break into; as though it's a ballerina
Frozen while trying to shift its weight
With a pirouette, a single flap
It will fill the void again with the sound of iridescent wings.

But it's much too late, it appears.
God's final desire to forgive died
A little while ago. Today, by winterlight
The desolate white sail
Torn from the clouds, lies in the water

The bird lies dead
Deep within winter the bird lies dead.

Nabaneeta Dev Sen

An academic, novelist, short-story writer, essayist, travel writer, and, of course, poet. Her prose has a light touch, and her poetry is feminist.

Festival 1992

The event is no longer under the manager's control

The moment one of them appears on the road with a rock
Two of us confront him with bricks
The instant one of us slumps in a pool of blood
With glittering eyes we fell seven of them
Bathing their bodies in blood
Those who would once rush to help the wounded
Are clapping now from their balconies
Someone's wife was taken away last night?
Let's strip all the women of the village in daylight
And drag them away too
Some bastard ripped out a boy's eyes?
Let us blind the entire country

A new festival of Rakhi Purnima starts now
We've made a glorious programme for Bhatridwitiya
Tethering heavy iron balls with protruding pins
To invisible chains, we will keep flagellating our chests
And with every breath and in every moment we will rent apart
All the three worlds with the silent sobbing of our souls
Oh my brother, oh my brother.

Lay your ear on the termite hill to hear the sounds

Like Gregor Samsa
One Morning

Like Gregor Samsa, one morning
Look, look how your world
Was changed too. You poor thing
Did you ever imagine it could be, would be, this way?
Did you ever think it would be so easy
So effortless to snap the bonds of life?

See how weightless your limbs are now
See how your ribs have melted to mush
The muscles can now be ripped
Like fluttering sheets of paper
If you're stabbed, not a drop
Of blood will fall

Later the maid will sweep out the dead vermin
And tuck it into the garbage pile

A Sparrow Once More

Don't ask me to be a fairy anymore
I cannot turn into a fairy at any hour at all
Moonlight frightens me, solitude is a deadweight
I beg of you
My heart has no moonbeams left
My mind is trussed up by sunlight
Let me
Be
A sparrow

The House

From one balcony to another, I keep escaping
From one room to the next. Just the one house
And a handful of rooms, fixed in number
And so I return in exhaustion to where I began.
No matter how seductively the painting on the wall
Smiles, the shadow on the floor is arrayed in combat.
How loudly people shout in this house, the glass
Is shattered, the vessels upset, furious arguments
Have broken out amongst the doors-windows-roof-
Walls-terrace of this house.
Fleeing from all of them
In complete fatigue, I spread the end of my sari
On the maddened floor and lie down on it.

Utpal Kumar Basu

Nature and Bohemianism are mingled in the work of this poet who began writing in the 1950s as part of the Krittibash group.

Signs of Joy and Sorrow No. 15

I perch on a tree. Eat its fruit. Fling its stone
At human beings. There's wailing below. I enjoy it.
Sometimes I sing classical tunes. They listen. Bring
Instruments. Keep time. Possibly take photographs too.
The other day
A researcher wanted a message. I thought I'd say: my life itself
Is my message. But apparently this has been said already. So
In my own way, a little twisted, I muttered
'I've seen mountains. And grown inscrutable.'

Signs of Joy and Sorrow No. 16

Let's go down to the fortress garden to play. The sun
Sets. Evening walkers merge into the sinking light.
Imperishable stone stands there, statues of soldiers
And several dangling tyres to swing on. Flocks of wild
Parrots are returning from the city. Even lower lies
The execution ground, the gallows, the iron cells
I hear shrieks, lamentation and elated birds. That's where
Our sport and songs of sport are today, our battle play.

Signs of Joy and Sorrow No. 32

Fearing the unknown sights I'll see on my morning walk in
the park
I start trembling at night, put the shoe on the wrong foot,
forget my
Umbrella, unfortunately the jeep that was in the accident is
still parked
Outside the police station, rusting, no air in its tyres, how
did the rope
Swinging from the tree get here, is it a noose, a pair of birds
fly out
Of the windows in the lock-up cell, they're nesting in the
mangled engine,
Eggless at the moment, without a child in their home, today
the day starts
With the darkness of storm-clouds, the rain is disorderly
now.

Shaileshwar Ghosh

Part of the Hungryalist Movement of poetry and literature from the 1960s.

I am Hungry

As soon as I put my hand on a woman's body she turned to
    gold
I'm a penniless labourer I live in Port Commission Quarter
    No. 5
The touch of my breath split the Communist Party into two
My arms lengthened, legs shortened, organ remained
    unchanged
I have seen my mother in bed with a god.

My father lost all he had gambling – an insane Van Gogh
Had seen flames in the rice fields and in Tahiti's islands
Gauguin's dog spread syphilis – from my mouth I have
    pulled out
The kind of sea whose tides don't swell, resist all attraction
Watching a boxing match on television I ran to my male
    friend.

I move around with you eat and drink with you sleep with
    you
I steal your money I buy one woman after another
When I enter a church its spire collapses, I am hungry
All the doors and windows of libraries close at my sight.

I was given hashish as payment for roasting the rotis
On the streets I hear nothing but my own footsteps
My words light up India's nuclear furnaces instantly
When I'm really upset I exchange blows with my friends
A friend stole ten rupees I didn't return a hundred I'd
    borrowed
I don't give a damn, for I have tasted heavenly flesh

Poetry rises like the Ochterlony Monument, destroying my
    mind
I tell the truth when I hallucinate – I see an angel

They're dismantled when struck by a rocket – when I'm
    hungry
They drag me away where my intestines fill with people's
    love
One of my mates is a bastard, another a traitor, one a
murderer
They escaped to our gathering without passports – another
    one
Broke into railway wagons to loot all the aluminium ovens
I take my girlfriend into the bathroom – I am blind in one
    eye
I have never seen a Rolls Royce – I like smoking by myself
And when necessary I push myself all the way to Dumdum
    Airport.

I plucked a single flower

I plucked a single flower it was enough to break my world
Every day I find my clothes ill-fitting on my body
I killed a bird whose song was meant to wake the world
I will be released after destroying every faith.
Memories of sleeping with her father figure makes a monk
    seek more darkness
The grass knows the lightning that strikes its breast is a play
    of power
At last I know that severing the stalk is the creator's finest act.

When there's celebration on the ground we're made to fear
    shipwrecks from a height
Our life is to watch, mesmerised, the male character playing
    the eunuch
An ascetic had to lay down his life because his heart had
    overflown with love
All the flowers that blossom from my deed are witches used
    to worship you.
I open my eyes to see the swan writhing in pain from the
    embedded arrow
When I nurse it back to life the hunter wants half of what
    I've saved
Peace descends only at those moments when gold and iron
    cost the same.
When I pluck the flower I'm a terrorist – I have offered my
    senses to the world
On the last train I heard the professional whore's
    enchanting singing with the thieves
All weapons are off on pilgrimage now – murderers have
    located their personal sorrows

The gods we have come to adore change their positions
 every day
Satan coils himself around a young girl like a serpent to
 drink from her breasts
The form in which I saw my mother from the womb burns
 bright in my memory
Life demands to know from life, are all forms of violence
 your children?

I plucked a single flower it was enough to break my world
A single tear falls on my face from space – I only gaze
 upwards
All the streams flowing from my body have gathered in a
 river
Many kicks await you still if the scars from the shackles
 remain
The moment terror was born, the world split into two,
 proponents and opponents
When the deluge begins every exponent of life seeks safe
 sanctuary.

Thrust your son into the wedding bedroom, father, stand
 guard with your stick
Over the iron bedroom, tonight he will be born and die
 soon after
The shortcut to heaven passes through hell.

I plucked a single flower it was enough to break my world
A droplet of light lay down its life to reveal the image of my
 darkness

Malay Roy Choudhury

One of the poets at the forefront of the Hungryalist
Movement of poetry and literature from the 1960s.

Insomnia

Writing comes on. I write.
Hunger comes on. I eat.
Love comes on. I love.
Agony comes on. I suffer.
Drunkenness comes on. I drink.
Laughter comes on. I laugh.
Touch comes on. I touch.
Seeing comes on. I see.
Cooking comes on. I cook.
Giving comes on. I give.
Reading comes on. I read.
Rest comes on. I rest.
Piss comes on. I piss.
Yawning comes on. I yawn.
Hate comes on. I hate.
Shit comes on. I shit.
Sneezing comes on. I sneeze.
Aching comes on. I weep.
Farting comes on. I fart.
Dancing comes on. I dance.
Singing comes on. I sing.
Breathing comes on. I am.

Sleep doesn't come on.
I don't dream.

Six Haikus

Spring in netherland
Swarms of bees knock at the door
The girl's floating corpse
~
Leaning out to see
The sky spread across the wind
Taillights just like blood
~
Her hands on her hips
Emperor Ashoka weeps
Black and freezing rocks
~
Crematorium
Coils of smoke and darting shrimps
The Buddha walks by
~
Someone's dead body
Hanging from the ceiling fan
There's a male spider
~
Memories of thieves
Tagore's slippers on the shelf
Much too large in size

Ketaki Kushari Dyson

Academician, novelist, poet, translator. Lives and writes in England. A Tagore scholar.

Fallen Leaves

There have been no letters from me -- such is your complaint.

I am compelled to tell you that if my disobedient letters were
once to start falling on your lap like the uncontrollable
leaves of autumn,
you wouldn't be able to cope with them, recipient.
Overflowing your lap into files, from files into drawers,
from drawers into the trunk,
finally pushing open the lid they would emerge in a
procession across the desk, the bed, the floor,
the doorstep, the top of the cupboard, the window ledge.
You would go mad.

The liberated leaves would not be contained even in your
empty room.
Unannounced, one night
without sending word I will reach your neighbourhood.
Peeping through the window I will see
suspended over the jumble of my letters smothering your room,
the white moon, laughing.

Your door is wide open.
Turned insane by the torrent of shed leaves, you have gone out
without locking your room.

I will see my letters lying there,
naked, helpless, weeping.
Anyone can pick them up and read them
and burst out laughing as they read:
in competition with the moon itself.

After the Rain

Clinging to the windscreen
And bonnet of a red car
Parked by the road
Is a profusion of wet flowers.
A sudden glimpse, a thudding heart.
They look like night-flowering jasmine.
Closer up, there's some doubt.
The petals probably belong to
Horse-chestnut blossoms.

There's no such tree nearby.
During the rain the car must have been parked
Beneath a horse-chestnut tree.

I circle the block in the direction
Where the tree stands.
From the grass I gather
A fistful of flowers – off-white
With a touch of red. I must compare.

The car has left.
Between my cold fingers
A clump of wet flowers
Like the agony of love
Smaller than the smallest
Greater than the greatest.

Nettle Tea

Very well, if that's what you want, I'll pluck nettles
With my bare hands and make nettle tea for you.
Even if they sting I won't rub crushed dock leaves on them.

But on one condition:
You'll have to stand nearby
As witness to the fact that I'm not using gloves.

Can you
Shoot a video
As documentation?

I'm telling you right now
I can't do it before the evening
Because first I must cook dinner.

After plucking nettles
I won't be able to work anymore:
My hands will sting.

Alternatively you could buy
Fish and chips from the local shop
Or whatever you prefer.

Serve yourselves dinner that night.
There'll be no need to set a place for me.
When doing the dishes,

Don't any of you forget to put on the rubber gloves,
Or else the scalding water and strong detergent
Will make your hands sting too.

One small request: please put
Elgar's Symphony No. 1 on the record-player.
Let the glass doors to the veranda be ajar.

While all of you eat
I will sit outside
And let my naked, lonely hands

Be bandaged gently by starlight
While I listen to the notes of the music
Make light of their burden

Like a row of experienced sherpas
And, with controlled footsteps,
Climb the mountain slowly.

~~~

Notes
In the wild, where nettles grow, dock leaves grow too. Nature
provides both the sting and the antidote to it. The phrase 'naked
lonely hands' is from a line in a poem by Jibanananda Das.

Beena Roy Sarkar

Progressive poet who made her mark in the 1960s and 1970s.

The Smell of Food

Everything in the country is changing swiftly
Still I feel hungry as soon as the sun rises
And so I can smell food in everything I see
Whenever I see a crowd I have the urge to rush
There must be some food where they're gathered
But I run up to them only to be disappointed
There's absolutely nothing for me over there
I wander around restaurants, rich people's homes
With hope in my heart, I might get a morsel
My hunger isn't quelled, only the smells grow sharper
I'm alive, I too know how to love and to hate
The dream of living shines in my eyes
I'm small but not insignificant, the spring passes
While I keep trying to find myself some food
The downtrodden and Dalits are certain to starve
Let there be a storm, let an apocalypse come
An apocalypse from which new men will emerge
I listen in hope for the footsteps of change
One nation, one heart, where all are equal
I sing the song of Ambedkar, who gave the call
For us to claim what is rightfully ours
Before I leave I will give up all I have
To the eternally deprived Dalit people

Shaheed Quaderi

A renowned poet from Bangladesh, known for his stirring, romantic lyrics.

A Salute to You My Love

Don't worry
I shall arrange it
So that the army
Marches past with bouquets
Of roses
And salutes you
My love.

Don't worry
I shall arrange it
So that armoured cars
With memories of many battlefields
Pass through forests
Cross barbed wires and barricades
And arrive laden with violins
Nowhere besides your doorstep my love.

Don't worry, I shall arrange it
So that the B-52s and Mig-21s
Drone overhead
Don't worry, I shall arrange it
So that chocolate, toffee and lozenges
Rain on you like paratroopers
In your courtyard alone my love.
Don't worry... I shall arrange it
So that a poet commands all the warships
In the Bay of Bengal
And in the next elections
Contesting against the war minister
A lover gets the entire popular vote

My love.
All possibilities of encounters, you can be sure,
Will end
I shall arrange it so that
A singer will become, unopposed,
The leader of the opposition
The trenches at the border
Will be guarded the year round
By red blue and golden hornets
Everything except the smuggling of love
Will be banned, my love.

Don't worry, I shall arrange it
So that inflation will drop and the number of poems
That surpass art every day will increase
I shall arrange it so that
The dagger will fall from the killer's hand
Out of fear not of collective anger
But of collective kisses
My love.
Don't worry
I shall arrange it
So that, like the guerrilla
Attack of spring on a winter park
Revolutionaries will line up in town
Playing accordions
Don't worry, I shall arrange it
So that roses
Or jasmines can be exchanged at the State Bank
For at least four hundred thousand taka
And one marigold will mean four cardigans
Don't worry, don't worry
Don't worry

I shall arrange it so that
The navy, army, and air-force
Will ring you and you alone from all
Sides and
Bow to you day and night, my love.

Deliver My Kisses

Young woman, your wild hair, suddenly undone
In a gust of mid-Manhattan wind
Plunging down on my chest
Like the eternal summer gale of Bengal
Reddened rainwater in your hibiscus eyes
Your imperilled breasts rocked like a sailboat
Amidst ragged waves
I hadn't imagined that such an extraordinary fire,
Apocalypse and destruction, were held in your kisses.
Young woman, I relinquish my rights to
The kisses being saved in secret
For my coppery, bitter lips and face
Leave me to the winter blizzards
In the exile I have chosen for myself
Let the season burning in the ice tear me apart like a pack of
    wolves
Only, you must
Deliver the hidden flames of my aroused kisses
To the weeping Bengal of June and July
Now on its knees, let my country ring with rolls of thunder.

Rafiq Azad

A renowned poet from Bangladesh, who described himself as a 'lover of humans, nature and romance'.

I'm Digging a Grave

I'm digging a grave
Digging for whom? – I don't know.

My parents are still alive,
I am certain they'll survive
For several years more – Not for them.

Although my only brother
Is a little ill, I would rather
See him live much longer – So not for him either.

My lonely sister, overcome
With grief for her dead husband – No, it's not for her.

Ever tolerant, ever humble
My wife, eternal safe harbour
For my storm-tossed soul – It isn't for her.

My joy, my happiness
My dearest children – Definitely not for them.

My lover, a sunflower
Her face turned to the sky – Nor is it for her.

I have not the slightest
Proclivity for suicide – And so it's not for myself

But it's true that
I'm digging a grave
For whom, then? – I don't know.

Manohar Mouli Biswas

A powerful voice of 'Dalit' literature from Bengal and India, he writes fiction, essays, and poetry.

Valmiki

You're an epic poet, Valmiki
In the eyes of Indians you're still an epic poet
By what power of art
Is your creation The Ramayana still an epic?
The blood that flowed through your veins
Was also Shambuka's
Didn't your hand shake even once when writing his murder?
You said children die prematurely
In immoral times
In your view a Shudra's attempts to be an ascetic was culpable
Severing the head of the man
Who hung upside down to perform the deepest penance
Did not make your hand tremble even a little
And, epic poet Valmiki, people across all of India
Still call you an epic poet

Mahadev Saha

One of the best-known modern romantic poets from Bangladesh, whose work is marked by high passion, while dealing with themes of solitude and yearning.

I Want

Today I want full-throated laughter
I want a summer storm, want madness
I do not want whispers and scandals
I want you to say it all out loud

Not tears or moisture, I want arid heat
I want burnt bridges and gaps that grow
I only want distance today, not intimacy
I don't want cooling shade, but a searing sun

Today I want baked clay, bricks, wood, iron
Mud and wild flowers, these are what I want
Today I want the roaring seas, violent waves
I want an earthquake that shatters the earth

I want a breast as open as the sky
I want fierce courage and infinite spirit
The tumult of the swift mountain river
I want a wild torrent, an explosion

I want separation today, not union
I do not want bonds, I want freedom
No more veils, I want to see and listen
I won't be anchored, I want to swim forever

I want to see

You show me the distant sky
A faraway world
But I want to see life round the corner
You want to show me inaccessible stars
Far-flung seashores
An extended horizon, remote mountains
You want to show me, even further away,
A romantic island, a tranquil lagoon
I only want to see this familiar lake
The river nearby
You want to show me the extended universe,
To take me close to eternity
My vision is limited
My eyes cannot see so far away
I only want to see the regions
That border on life
Leave the distant stars alone, show me
The map of proximity
Show me the river bank, the vine on the roof
The front yard
Not distant mysteries, I only want to unravel
Your heart

Bhaskar Chakrabarti

Made his mark in the 1960s. The title poem of his book, *When Will Winter Come Suparna* has become something of a legend.

When will Winter Come, Suparna?

When will winter come, Suparna, I'll sleep for three
    months— every evening
Someone plays a prank and transfers frog blood
Into my body, I sit in silence in the darkness
Some people set a blue balloon flying, there are fireworks
    all night
Celebrations, and then suddenly
All the candles go out together like magic, the festive day
Is blown away somewhere else like the wind, the whistles
Can no longer be heard, when I see water I want to plunge in
I feel an urge to submerge myself in it
And breathe with my head out of the water, I hate it, Suparna,
I am not like humans, nor like light or dreams, my feet
Are growing broader all the time, the moment I hear the
    clatter of hooves
My heart trembles, I raise my face to breathe, I move the hands
Of the clock forward with my fingers, I hate it, when
Will winter come, Suparna, I'll sleep for three months
Once I saw, as soon as I woke at dawn, the clouds leaning
Near the window, darkness everywhere
I couldn't even see my own nails clearly that day
Weeping when I remembered you, I took a match to my head,
Falling asleep again to the smell of burning hair
I am no longer human now, walking down the road, I
Feel the urge to leap suddenly, I no longer like sitting
Submissively before love for a long three months, whenever
I hear human footsteps
My breath turns ragged, I run away in the direction I came
    from Why do I run? I hate it
When will winter come, Suparna, I'll sleep for three months

Tangles

A life of mistakes like a ghost a death of mistakes like a
    ghost is toying with me
What's the date today is it Monday or Tuesday I'm trying to
    find out and I just can't remember just can't
The sweet and broken and crumpled faces are hovering
    over the streets now
I can see why melancholy sank its teeth into me at nineteen
    and my head is beginning to hang with shame
What's the date today my breath is still circulating in our
    suburbs although this room is tiny now and the days are
    damaged and the nights have no cracks
Full of happiness a fresh young woman's face of sixty-two
    or sixty-three so many smiles smiling in silence and
    glasses
and writing her self-satisfied diary
Where did the explosion take place melancholy I let you
    mingle with my blood when I was just nineteen
A narrow boat sailed past every afternoon where were my
    eyes where my education when on the frozen table
    electric shocks devoured my mind
Careful death a dangerous gentleman brought a telegram
    My head is beginning to hang with shame
Am I forgetting my burnt orange dreams I cannot
    remember I am racing down B.T. Road my teacher is
    saying I mustn't pause for breath when reciting
    declensions
Why can't I wander around at night a learned and ancient
    philosopher was born today in the torrential rain
Full of happiness a fresh young woman's face so many
    smiles smiling in silence and glasses and hands in repose

On a summer morning through a bus window our city our
Calcutta keeps drifting keeps drifting
Someone said who was it who said the rain will be on the
next tram I cannot remember I cannot remember all day
and all night my nerves whisper
When fingers keep groping for a relationship in the empty
postbox
When I observe as I lie in the belly of a gigantic python
My funeral procession moving towards the crematorium
slowly while I follow.

The Language of Giraffes

1
How swiftly the years race away
At dusk a face or two floats up
My friends are resting
Far away
In my life only leaves are shed

2
My existence is a hospital
So I've often thought in the noonday sun
In the after-afternoon, when life
Is drowsy
No one, nothing, seems to exist, near and far

3
Because you'll come, I've snagged a wicker chair
I wonder, will you come? Will you really come?
Two decades have passed – or four? I still sit in the darkness
Why this loneliness, why this pulse in my veins
You are mild (fragrant air), peace, peace in my nerves,
Panacea.

Nirmalendu Goon

A poet from Bangladesh whose works are deceptively accessible, marked by sensuality, an eye for nature, distinctive ideas, and an eternally youthful sensibility.

I am Earth

I am earth. All this while
I wasn't sure, but now I'm certain
I am earth. If I weren't earth
Why do these buds blossom
All night long in my fists?

I am earth. If I weren't earth
Why do these flowers blossom
All night long in my fists?
I don't know about daylight, but at night I am earth

The Pebble

One day on the beach, long ago,
I found and took away a tiny pebble
How old was I then? Thirty-two?
You were nineteen or, at most, twenty

My overwhelmed heart was occupied with it
But now I want that lost pebble back
Where's the pebble? Where's my tiny pebble?
It's playing hide and seek in the sea

Scouring seven oceans, not just one
I know how hard it will prove to find
But still I look for it in my madness
I can never shake it from my mind

A sudden pain in my guts one day
It was in my gall-bladder, said the x-ray
The doctors advised me to cut it off
But I simply couldn't find a way
I feared the knife, they thought. But I said
It's my private wealth, let it stay
Why are your eyes so red?

I'm not saying I have to be loved,
I want someone to wait for me
Just to open the door when I come
I'm tired of unlocking the door for myself

I'm not saying I have to be loved
I want someone to lay out a meal
There's no need to fan me as I eat

I know that the age of electricity
Has freed woman from serving her man
I want someone to ask me whether
I need a glass of water, or some salt
Whether I'd like another roasted chilli
To go with the fritters on my plate
I can wash my own dishes and clothes

I'm not saying I have to be loved
I want someone to open the door for me
Someone to tell me to eat a little
If not a companion in lust and desire
Someone to ask, 'Why are your eyes so red?'

Firearms

The police station is crowded, suspicious soldiers
Are collecting firearms. Under military orders
The shotguns, rifles, pistols and cartridges of cowards
Are like flowers on a table offered at the shrine for louts
Only I, disobeying the commands of the Army, have turned
Into a tender rebel – I return home in full view, and yet I hold
A firearm as dangerous as the heart, I haven't turned it in

Phalguni Roy

Part of the Hungryalist Movement of poetry and literature from the 1960s.

I have no conflict with people

No, I have no conflict with people any more
I can easily take my creditor to the hospital if he's in an
    accident
I can unhesitatingly ask my old lover's husband for a
    cigarette
As easily as growing a beard I can now see
A universal sexual peace in Ramakrishna's devotion to Kali
When I lose a single slipper I buy a new pair
No, I have no conflict with people any more

My uncomfortable gaze shifts from my sister's breasts
On the ritual day of sisterly love I wander around
    whorehouses
When I die I will see the corridor of second births
Till the moment before my birth I didn't know I would be
    born
I am a man without redemption engaged in destiny
I am a man without destiny engaged in terrorism
I have seen a dog sobbing within me constantly
For his bitch, a monk become an eager debauch
To take his female counterpart's self-imposed virginity
And even heavenly love is pulverised by this seduction
Eventually I'm in favour of seeking the joy of life
Instead of rhythm in poetry, that's why I have no conflict
With life, no conflict with people

A redundant poem

I am a newly arrived stranger on earth's ancient body
Now as the doctor slices the poet's vein to let the blood drip
I remember wanting to sell my own blood
To drink and write poetry
Have I become dissolute? Many mysteries are still under cover
I am still afraid to die, which means I love life
So I walk beneath the overcast sky
With the Red Book in one hand and Jibanananda's poetry
In the other – I dislike those who wear sunglasses
When it's cloudy, I dislike those who think of god
When slammed by the world, I adore those who kick away
Idols of the deities and ask what is what, with great enthusiasm
I take Marx Lenin Sartre Joyce Kafka to the Coffee House
To destroy cigarettes and then walk by myself through a crowd
Of people, desolate, actually I'm getting nothing from books
Hoping to get something from my lover I run to her
To find her in bed with my elder brother, an officer, I am
    unemployed
I talked of love with the whores, my brother the officer bought
My lover a sari with his bonus and became her lover, the money
He spent would have paid for my meals for a month, which
    means
It costs the same to cover my future wife's body and to feed me
Can you imagine this existence of ours
Still I love the naked child's giggles, the renewal of the
Ancient earth, before my hungry eyes the beautiful woman's
Framework of bones passes through time towards the pyre,
    I sell
Fat philosophy books to buy bread and alcohol just for
    sustenance
I even manage to write, believe me, a redundant poem

Debarati Mitra

Began writing in the 1960s. A worthy successor to Kabita Sinha as a feminist poet.

Applied Mathematics

That two and two are four
Is not something I believe anymore
Mixing two with two might make a piglet
Or even the Manhattan Project that spawned the nuclear bomb.
There's the sun disappearing in the river
Like a fish breaking free of the rod and line,
And that boy there is plucking cabbage
Making a shadow parallel to the horizon.
A train chugs up
Entering its ambit
All of this adding up to a late afternoon
But there's no connection between them.
A woman and a man have been talking for 45 minutes
They can't possibly be husband and wife
Or everyday lovers.
Not bother and sister, or even the flower and the rain
What then?
I don't want to calculate the speed of the wind
Nor the clock's.

Will adding the colour blue to the flight-path of the bird
Make the sky?
Will adding a sigh to the reflection in the mirror
Make it me?
Not all caterpillars + two wings
Equal the butterfly.

Observing all this
I flung the new applied mathematics book I've written
Up in the sky
A star of advancing years
Leafing through its pages, blinking,
Exclaimed: Atheist.

Tunnu's Computer

Dorothy Smith of South Africa had set my data
Whether I'm woman or man, creature or matter
She alone knows
I am alive, though
I even think of myself as a woman
I was placed inside
A Blue G royal faber machine
Then, bouncing between places
I'm in Tunnu's hands now
Tunnu skips her classes at school
Plays the synthesiser
Dances with her friends
She doesn't play games herself, but watches
And operates her computer sometimes.

Actually I'm an awkward robot
Halfway through a game
I don't know yet how the story ends
It seems there's a princess in a kingdom
A harassed Tunnu sends me off to find her
Blowing up a pillar, she makes me climb
A cloud in an instant
The next moment I'm swimming, breathless,
With mermaids seven hundred miles under the sea
Rummaging in the freezing sand of the desert for her
She must be in a room in the palace
An immense mirror in front of her
I am forced to shatter it
A part of her soul spills over to this side
Mrs Smith hadn't meant for me to suffer so

But Tunnu doesn't care
It's all a game to her.
One day Tunnu, Bisku and Lyree
Were playing on the computer in the living room
Her friends told her
Change your computer games, Tunnu
So boring and so immature
We'll copy some intelligent games for you
From the Rainbow Research Centre

My foolish body began to tremble at this
I was almost extinguished, sobbing
Press any key you like, I'm not
Going to respond to your juvenile wishes anymore
Instead I made her hand
Shake and jerk
And bend like a bough

Dr Smith had never even dreamt of such a thing.

Humayun Azad

The most renowned among Bangladesh's progressive poets and writers, with enormous influence on poets and writers who followed.

I will probably die for something very small

I will probably die for something very small
For a tiny rainflower
For a tottering dewdrop
Perhaps I will die for a petal
Fluttering in the April breeze
For a bead of rain

I will probably die for something very small
For a robin's song
For a dimple on a baby's cheek
Perhaps I will die for a single tear
Glistening in someone's eye
For a pearl of sunlight

I will probably die for something very small
For a sliver of moonlight
For a fragment of a cloud
Perhaps I will die for a butterfly
Lost on the twenty-first floor of a tower
For a speck of green

I will probably die for something very small
For an infinitesimal dream
For a trifling sadness
Perhaps I will die for a short-lived sigh
In someone's sleep
For a drop of beauty

On the Death of My Lover

I feel on top of the world Lilian,
Constant explosions will shatter me no more.
Blinded and misled by the waves, the ship
Will now negotiate the calm waters.
Someone is draining the saliva from the lips
Gouging the flesh to excavate diamonds;
Earth will no longer shake with these fears.
Jungle fires and thunderclaps will cease.

Slowly the moon will begin to burn today,
Daily life will turn supremely healthy.
Rice, water, fragrance will taste fresh again,
The enemy's face will reveal my friends.
I'll know that night was always meant for sleep,
Those whom slumber shuns can only sing.
Warm blood seeks to fill the chilled coffin,
I feel on top of the world Lilian.

Nabarun Bhattacharya

A legendary poet and writer of the 1970s and afterwards. His urban subaltern characters and use of street language mark him out as a unique writer.

This Valley of Death
is Not My Land

The father who fears identifying his son's corpse
Is someone I hate
The brother who still behaves brazenly naturally
Is someone I hate
The teacher, intellectual, poet and clerk
Who do not want to avenge this killing in public
Are people I hate
Eight dead bodies
Lie blocking the road that reason takes
I am losing my head
Eight pairs of staring eyes glare at me in my sleep
I scream
They keep calling me to the garden at ungodly hours
I'll go mad
Kill myself
Do whatever the hell I want
On walls with stencils in manifestos this is the time to write
    poetry
With one's own blood, tears and bones, the collage
technique
Can be used to compose poetry right now
With a face torn apart by piercing agony
Staring unflinchingly at the blinding headlight of the van
Confronting terror
Poetry can be flung at the world right now
The .38s and whatever else the assassins have
Can all be ignored and poetry can be read immediately
In the stone-cold lock-up cell
Shaking the light beam of the autopsy

In the courtroom presided over by the murderer
In the institutions of lies and miseducation
Within the state machinery of oppression and terror
In the heart of military and civil authorities
Let the protest of poetry be echoed
Let the poets of Bengal too
Prepare, like Lorca
For murder, strangulation, missing corpses
Let them prepare to be riddled by stengun bullets
Still it is essential
That village poetry surrounds city poetry
This valley of death is not my land
This stage for the executioner's exultation is not my land
This vast crematorium is not my land
This blood-soaked slaughter-house is not my land
I will snatch my land back
I will hold in my arms the dew-kissed reeds and autumn
Fireflies all over my head or harvests on mountain slopes
Innumerable hearts grains fairytales flowers women rivers
I will name each of the stars for a martyr, as I wish
I will draw to me the tottering breeze the fisheye lake
Love, from which I've been exiled a lightyear away since
        birth
I will call it to myself the day we celebrate the revolution
I reject
Interrogations under blinding thousand-watt beams all day
        and night
I reject
Needles thrust beneath nails, being laid on slabs of ice
I reject
Being hung by the feet till blood pours out of the nose
I reject
Boots stamping on lips, wounds everywhere from red-hot rods

I reject
Pouring alcohol on skin lacerated by spiked whips
I reject
Electric shocks on naked bodies, grotesque sexual torture
I reject
Death by beating, being shot dead by a gun held to the head
Poetry admits no barriers
Poetry is armed poetry is free poetry is fearless
Look at us, Mayakovsky Hikmet Neruda Arragon Eluard
We have not allowed your poetry to be defeated
The entire land is trying to write an epic poem
All rhetoric is about to be composed to a guerrilla rhythm
Let the drums and castanets reverberate
Let tribal villages turn the indigo fields
Crimson with blood like coral islands
Poisoned by the foamy venom of the king cobra
The death-drenched river thirsty wolf's bane
Blinded sun twanging string of a mythical bow
Arrows fired with vicious arrowheads
Boatman with your battle-axe
Flashing spears lances to occupy the island
Tribal totems with bloodshot eyes dancing to drumbeats
Guns scythes daggers and mountains of courage
So much of it that there's no fear
Convoys of bulldozers with bared teeth and cranes
Mobile dynamos turbines lathes and engines
Diamond-hard eyes in the methane darkness of sliding coal
Hammers of miraculous steel
Thousands of fists in docks jute mills furnaces punching the
    air
No I am not afraid
The ashen face of fear is a stranger's
When I know death is nothing but love.

If I am murdered
I will spread as the flame in every earthen lamp in Bengal
I cannot be destroyed
From the earth I will emerge as green comfort year after
    year
I cannot be destroyed
I will live in joy in sorrow in birth in funerals
As long as Bengal exists
As long as humans exist
The death that ascends like a blazing bubble on a cold night
Bring that day that battle that end of life
Let the mercantile voyager stop the Seventh Fleet in its path
Let the war be heralded by the bugle and the horn
When the air is intoxicated by the scent of blood
Let poetry ignite the gunpowder to explode the soil
When murals villages boats towns temples
From the Terai to the edges of the Sundarban
Are dry and combustible after weeping all night
When the birthplace and the slaughterhouse are one
Then what doubts
Why the hesitation
Have the eight of them touched the terror
Are they whispering in the darkness of acceptance
To ask who's standing guard and where
Their voices hold a million constellations the Milky Way
The inherited right to float between planets
Let the burning torch of poetry
Let the Molotov Cocktail of poetry
Let the toluene flames of poetry
Throw themselves at this desire for fire.

For You, For Me, For Us

You can beg for forgiveness
Knock your head on the floor, weeping
Sign an affidavit stating
You will never be courageous again
Or you can choose a hospital bed
Or vomit blood at noon
Whichever you prefer
But a system has branded you
On your back with a heated rod
Death's number is on my back too
We look like the inmates
Of a concentration camp
Though the barbed wire
Isn't visible to the naked eye
Someone keeps chanting the numbers
Though they cannot be heard
Everyone must consider what's to be done
The branches cast a shadow like a cross
Where there's a cross, there are people
To be nailed to it, and people to drive the nails
Through their hands and feet
And since everything is inevitable,
Predestined and inexorable
Then why should we not scream once
Why should we not try just once
To be independent, unfettered, free
What else is there to do
For you, for me, for us,
Countrymen?

Helal Hafiz

Poet and writer from Bangladesh whose verses were used for graffiti during the liberation war.

Domestic Politics

If all the arrangements for love have failed
Come to the next procession
In slogans our conversation will be veiled

During this famine love on the street if you will
Should you bring a perfect desire
Come dressed in your red sari, still

The Snail

'Marvellous, marvellous!'
Shouted some people in unison.
The eldest snail in town,
I coiled up afresh after stirring once
The way I'd been coiled
Across watery latitudes
The way I'd lurked inside, spruce and trim,
Approaching human beings,
I grew desolate in a new pose
Again I was alone, as I had been alone before.

Parthapratim Kanjilal

Has been both a pioneer and a significant influence in Bengali poetry, writing within the frame of unorthodox poetry while at the same time building a significant readership despite, or perhaps because of, his remoulding of the language.

Unemployment, Postmodern

I've lost my job. After which money keeps pouring in
A cordless phone is here – the TV's been upgraded –
This one's actually a flatscreen LED set –
Where's all this coming from? I don't have my job –
I won't get another one at this age, hardly had I said
This on the phone when two or three cheques came. For
    what?
For writing? But I don't write, I've not been the greatest
    writer
Of any of the past decades – yet, is it for my writing?
Not so! One of the bosses at the company I left
Told me when I met him on the street, the way you
Deconstructed your job is unique! I too want to give you
A gift – please, accept it and remember me by it –
And yet it was he who got the lion's share of my work,
It can be stated clearly. In my job, somehow
I had managed to rise just above the lower middle-class
But my ways now are upper-class – and yet I do nothing
I have no job but a buckets of anxiety,
Moving around the city in search of a job
I spend a thousand on taxi fare every day
Negotiations are underway to buy a flat –
I have no job, no work – but a healthy income
People protest in unison when I tell them I'm unemployed
Of course, we know that, you don't have to tell us
And then the money keeps rushing in – I have, meanwhile,
Written to the papers asking for a job to be donated
The way people donate eyes – the government, the
    opposition,
Extremists, the UN – they're all considering my plea.

Joy Goswami

The poet who, along with Shakti Chattopadhyay, epitomises the post-Jibanananda Das era of Bengali poetry. Arguably the finest poet in the language at present. Also a writer of novels and drama in verse, as well as prose.

We're happy with crumbs

We're happy with crumbs
Why bother with sadness?
We can spend our lives
With ordinary clothes and food

Our lives go past us
In illness and in debt
At night my brother and I
Smoke cannabis

We can't afford food every day
When we shop we overdo it
On our way back home
We buy rose seedlings

But where to plant them?
Can we be sure they'll bloom?
All that will come later
We smoke cannabis now

We're happy with crumbs
Why bother with sadness?
We can spend our lives
With ordinary clothes and food

Sometimes the day just stops
We come home at midnight
Rage overtakes the meal
There's no salt in the cold rice

I'm overcome by fury
I overcome my fury
Father and two sons
We scream in the streets

And what if we do?
We're ordinary people
Let there be arrangements
For salt in our rice

To the Rulers

I will do
Exactly what you want
Eat what you want
Wear what you want
Bathe in what you want before I go out
Without demurring
If you ask me I'll hang by the neck all night
From a noose
But when you tell me the next day
To climb down
Other people will have to lower me
I won't be able to do it alone
Because I couldn't do that last bit
Don't think I disobeyed you.

How certain how lightning how deer this run is today

How certain how lightning how deer this run is today
How expanse, how flying dust this arm

How peacock this dance

How pit how closed how tongue lolling this envy
How inevitable graves all the cavities
And how sudden sinking the pursuing ghouls

How empress this rhythm is today
Which not even the devil can imagine buying

Anita Agnihotri

Acclaimed and sensitive writer of both poetry and fiction, chronicler of the lives of people on the margins.

The mother's on her way

The boy sleeps in the rickshaw, there's his mother
Her hand supporting his neck; the rickshaw wobbles
Chest perspiring, he mutters in his sleep, homework
Project-work for tomorrow, there's his mother
At home she will cook; there's a curry in the fridge
Sweep the floor, put yesterday's clothes out in the sun
The boy's father is on a nasty assignment in Tinsukia
People seldom return from that place. The neighbour
Has refused to look after the little girl, she can barely crawl
And yet I give her sugar every day, lend her flour
The son sleeps in the rickshaw, when will he wake up
Or grow up, make his mother ride pillion with him
To show her his workplace, the hair at her temples
Is greying, like the winter sunlight the mother's youth
Dwindles in the wind, the girl who crawls today
Will go to school. When the father's home on vacation
He stays home, always sleeping, won't help
With a thing around the house. He wants to rest.
The mother's on her way, the road just won't end
For either the mother or the rickshaw-driver.

The Butterfly's Lifespan

How long is a butterfly's lifespan? How long?
A siris tree will live many years more
Rivers will exist longer still, as for mountains
There's no counting their age.

Winging through the constant cooing of a dove
On a wet, cloudy day, has the butterfly ever wondered
How much longer, how much?

The butterfly has seen the rainbow slice through the rain
To be born, but it too has vanished in the glare of sunlight
The butterfly lives longer than a rainbow.

As it flies very close to the sun-scorched earth
The warmth in its breast grazed by blades of grass
The butterfly has no idea the colours on its wings
Ebb and flow in monsoon and in spring
Or when the call will come
Out of the blue
As it flies, there's just the one flower
That the butterfly searches
As soon as it alights on the petals the butterfly remembers
Nothing else.

Subodh Sarkar

Started writing poetry towards the end of the 1970s. Constructs his verse with techniques of prose, creating a unique form of 'unpoetic' poetry.

Rich People Poor People

Rich people never see
The light of dawn
Likewise, poor people never say 'good morning'
Rich people's daughters
Go to Mauritius to sunbathe
Poor people's yards
Are sunbaked into boats.
Rich people cannot
Go to bed before midnight.
Poor people fall asleep, starving, at seven-thirty
In their sleep they dream
Of a slum in their empty stomachs
Of a fourteen-storeyed building
In full bellies.
The slum is telling the fourteen-storey
Crumble to the ground and die
I'll take your doors for use
In the slum.
The fourteen-storeyed says, burn to ashes
I'll build fourteen storeys on top of you.

Did You Say Globalisation?

I went to America and heard
People there are also saying
What times are these we live in
If you don't get to your food
At the right time
Someone else will get to it.
But this is what the poor
Used to do in our country.
Now, because there are three harvests a year
One thinks twice before snatching
A meal from a beggar or a madman.
But yesterday I heard
An MNC executive Angshuman
Roy
Was, how wonderful, sent en famille
To Mauritius for a holiday.
Ten days later he returned to find
Sitting in his chair
A little fairer than him
A little taller
With a thicker head of hair, another
Angshuman Roy.

Pinaki Thakur

Began writing poetry in the 1980s. Colloquial cadences
and an inherent romanticism are his distinctive qualities.

The Friend

A mechanical man from a lost planet is in our house today
The dust from the lost planet cakes his machine-made feet,
A man, a man – but in fact he lacks some human traits
His complexion? His smile? Two blue bulbs in his eye sockets?

Oh yes… that's right… somewhere… there's something…
　　strange
Odd (like in the comics) behaviour I've noticed, he never asks
Your name or offers you chocolate in return for your
　　friendship
(Besides, you saw, Didi? The robot, a-ha, didn't ask for water.)

And so a mechanical man from a lost planet is visiting us
Licks his plate clean, takes showers too, but doesn't sleep
So much conversation and music on tapes inside him
Just keep saying hmm all day. It'll work. But he'll fail a quiz.

Did you take a train here? Or a taxi? No idea. It's possible
That the moment I dreamt Superman was gone, that he had
　　died—
He captured my tears from thought waves and got the
　　spacecraft
To land on our terrace, and will now say, 'I am ET…'

There, he's smiling. Ma smiles too. Robots have metal hearts.
He doesn't say thanks, didn't laugh on hearing my name's
　　Enfant

Tell me, Didi, don't robots have enfants of their own?

Mallika Sengupta

Poet and academician. Began writing a unique brand of robust feminine poetry in the 1980s. Even as a Marxist she could question Marx, 'Will women be the handmaids of the revolution?'

While Teaching My Son History

'History is nothing but man's activity
In pursuing his aims'
~ Karl Marx, *The Holy Family*

From history we have come to know all this
The first human was Java Man, Cro-Magnon
Neanderthal Man, all of them barbarians
Surviving by battling with nature
Killing bears with blunt stone weapons
Blowing into reeds to play the flute
They created this man-made civilisation
Shadow women by their sides, or not

When Paleolithic Man stepped aside
All humans were Stone Age men
Iron Age men moulding the hard metal
All these ancient people were men
From history we have come to know all this

The forefathers were alone, mankind too
We have no womankind, nor foremothers
History is his story of sperm and valour
Because it makes no reference to women
We know women did not exist then

Man was born in the womb of Java Man
Neanderthal Man fed children at his breast
Java and Neanderthal Men were only male
The man alone was both god and goddess

The male mother was the male father
The male was both melody and flute
The male was both penis and uterus
From history we have come to know all this

The historian was in fact a eunuch

Pandu's Desire for Sons

[Two and a half thousands years later
Sex will be determined on earth
Its name, amniocentesis.
~ So astrologers said]

We want only sons
Let the infant smell of sons pervade the green earth

Pandu said, sons are of many kinds
My own son will be of my own seed
But if not, I depend on you, my partner in duty
Lie with the man I choose, create a son for me
Or I can buy the precious sperm of a man
A son will be conceived in your body

The woman's womb-soil seeks a plough
If I am impotent, I shall hire, or employ
Or by any other means bring you seed, Kunti,
Grain-goddessm fill my arms with your harvest

Kingly joys or wealth and fame, I want none of it
I do not want the birth of a daughter, we want only sons

Salt

Cordelia had loved like a grain of salt
Her aged father whose name was Lear
Salt is a marvellous object on earth
Of miraculous form, fragrance and essence
A pinch of salt makes noble rice immortal
Gurgling with warm water needs some salt
Infected eyes too. Salt is ubiquitous
Still, there's danger in salt
Listen to the warning signs in every clinic
Too much salt in your food will raise blood-pressure
Fat or thyroid.
Bengalis asked for nothing but salt and rice
Still saltwater sweeps away the delta islands
Fishing villages are eaten by saline flows.
Life without salt leaves you shivering in cold
Yet salt kills leeches, it kills only leeches!
Anguished midwives in Bihar's villages
Stuff balls of salt into newborn girls' throats
And close their mouths, for twenty-five rupees
Just twenty-five rupees and a wave of hatred
For the unwanted girl. Grains of salt
Turn apocalyptic. Hundreds of Cordelias
Are murdered by death-dealing salt

Kalyani Thakur Charal

A poet from the 1990s who is most comfortable in her skin as a 'Dalit' poet. Her poetry expresses the anguish of 'Dalit' women.

The Woman in the Darkness

Whisper to the moonlight
The story of the woman
Who measures the darkness
Even the fireflies
Know of the woman
In the corner of the house
The woman who breaks the silence
Has the deer
As her friend
The clouds know
The despair
Of the woman drenched in the rain
The woman who swims
Against
The current
Never has her sail torn
By storms in October
The woman who grinds spices
Has the mortar and pestle
As companions
The spices know her tongue
Ginger and chilli and cummin and poppy
She's like a miracle
That strong woman
Who wipes her sweat and lifts
Along with the primitive yoke
The ruby in the darkness

A Dialogue Between the Oppressor and the Oppressed

This anguish over them
The revolution seems an indulgence to you people
Grilling their votes for eating
Is also our job
At least we know what's going on with them the year round
Why have you people suddenly decided
To put up a show of revolution right now

We're ignorant people who don't understand, sahib
The two of you are our god
Before your eyes our boy is sacrificed
God of sacrifices
How much blood must flow to satisfy you
Go away from where you watch over us
We'll die of starvation, even that's better
It will save the lives of our children
We don't need development, all that is for you
What happens in the forest
What has happened for thousands of years in the forest
Has not killed us
Don't take our blood for your development, god
You are kings who fight one another
While poor men die
Our wounds are deeper at this age
We remember the zamindar's soldiers
So many lives given up to protect the land
O revolutionary friends descended from zamindars
The same game by a different name and colour
Still makes so much blood flow

Mandakranta Sen

This 1990s poet was the first after Joy Goswami to introduce new rhythms to Bengali poetry. She fuses a leftist sensibility with feminist individuality.

The Story of the Arjun and the Krishnachura

The Arjun tree stood alone in that field
An Aryan male – a pillar of aristocracy
All the other trees bowed to it
This was merely the beginning of the story

From somewhere came the Krishnachura seed
A few years later she was a young woman
A Santhal girl, with crimson in her hair
At once Arjun wanted her as his own

She was not a girl who would submit
In spring she dressed up without help, alone
She wasn't drawn to the Aryan male
She was busy making the buds bloom

Last night's flowers had fallen from her hair
Rippling leaves had woven clothes for her
Arjun – he was an Aryan male, who thought
Only he could claim beauty so fair

From the distance the Arjun tree could see
The Krishnachura's cascading heart
Bewitched by beauty, his perplexed eyes
Wondered when he'd find his way to it

I'd better finish this story quickly
The Krishnachura is far too obstinate
Her pride won't let her sell herself
She'd rather be a neighbour or a friend

The story isn't quite so simple
Arjun shed his bark, sheds it still
But the Santhal girl can shed blood
The Aryan male accepts he cannot win

Be reborn as an Arjun tree
Consider the Krishnachura a friend
Don't confuse me with others, upright one
When I bleed, shed your bark and call me then

A Foreign Land

Wait, before being torn and ripped
Let me memorise your lips
The border of grass beyond
The lips; the slightly fragile
Intensity; the danger-engendering
Heat; the irresistible, excellent
Rain; so much of it, so much
And, on this bursting summer day,
From the northwest corner of your lips
A storm arrives

I stand with my feet on the frontier
Within our lips there's a growth of
Barbed wire. Suppose I'm dying to visit
Your lips today, I think it will
Take many years. Still, tell me
Try to remember and then tell me
What was it that really changed
After our lips were partitioned
Besides our kisses?

The Heart's a Disobedient Girl

The heart's a disobedient girl
Don't explain her studies to her
Her textbooks are ripped, with her spit she has
Rubbed off the indelible script of fate
In the blue grammar book
She's scribbled boys' names
Even their pictures
The heart's a disobedient girl
You want to punish her? She won't care

Rajani

Just Rajani's luck
Any man she likes
They're all married

Her aunt told her yesterday
If you heart awakes from sleep
It's proper to raise your eyes

What's the use of doing that
Saris dry in their garden
Playing in that arbour is wrong

Still the full moon is the sky's guest
She climbs to the roof, a silent urge
Mesmerised by moonlight, the girl

You'll jump, Rajani, won't you?

Srijato

The best among contemporary young poets. His work lays claim to an experimental uniqueness in its use of language, rhythm and structure.

My Parents and I

A

I never got to visit Puri with my father and mother
Nor Shimla or Ooty.
Never mind those distant places, we didn't even go to the
    zoo or the book fair
I only got back home, switched on the light, entered
My own room and observed
How, adding to their mutual distance every day
My father and mother made room for me to go away

B

On some nights the force of gravity stops working in our
    locality
When I'm late getting home, I start floating on the road,
Dogs, cats, rickshaws all float past me. Somehow I manage to
Open the front door and find the food strewn on the floor
    while
The crockery is happily floating about and among them my
    mother
Floats too, her head on my father's shoulder... no
    annoyance,
No squabbles or catfights... as though I haven't even been
    born yet,
The house redolent with the aroma only of peace and joy. In
    happiness
And embarrassment I float too in a corner of the kitchen,
    falling asleep
Slowly till things return to normal, till their bitter quarrel
    awakens me

C

My mother has many demands
She wants me to be a great poet, get a job
Have a happy marriage
And many other small things
My father doesn't want anything anymore.
Slower and more hunched by the day, my father's needs
Amount to three matchsticks every night.
One to light a cheap cigarette
And two, just in case my mother and I are lost

D

My father was once a great friend of mine
My mother, my friend's wife
Then, as is usually the case
The friend grows distant
His wife comes closer
For instance, my father now
Sits idly on the stairs
My mother and I
Chat, watch TV, go to bed together

E

Newspaper doors? Shut
TV channel doors? Shut
School and college doors? Shut

Only the door home is open. So I go home.
My mother is teaching music downstairs. Songs of a lifetime.
I slink into my own room and lie down.
Very late at night, when it's almost dawn, I tiptoe
Into my mother's room next to mine and sink my teeth into
    her sleeping throat

No songs. Warm, fresh blood.
And, incapable of sinking his teeth into anyone, my father,
Locked out of work ten years ago, sits silently at a distance
    on the floor holding a cup. Waiting.

F

My father and mother have this cat-like thing
About them. Much of the day they curl up
In corners, their eyes closed. When awake
They bicker over fish curry and milk packets,
Hurling ever louder yowls at each other
Even taking swipes with their paws
How long can one stand this? I'm tempted
To take them by the scruffs of their necks
Abandon them somewhere, that'll teach them.
But then I think, they aren't really cats,
At their age they may not be able to
Find their way back home anymore.

G

I believe my father ran away to Puri when he fell in love
With my mother. Because she had turned him down at first.

In Puri, sitting by the ocean
My father gobbled slices of fried fish and drank copiously
While my mother, with a high head of hair and large eyes
Mused on the way back from college, why didn't I say yes

This year in Puri I really wanted to
Locate that storm-blown father of mine
Bring him back to Calcutta to stand
By my mother, just turned twenty-five
But when I asked the locals they said

All that isn't available anymore
The sea has retreated a long way in these thirty years

H
Perhaps I was asleep one day and my father had gone out
When my mother's old lover came and said on seeing me
—Which class is he in now?

Perhaps I was asleep again another day and my mother had
    gone out
When my father's old lover came and said on seeing me
—He's just like you

Awake now after all these years
I'm looking for those two again

Did they ever meet?
Fall in love?
Did they marry and settle outside the city?

Couldn't I go and live with them?

I
And after all this, bearing my father and mother on my
    shoulders
I pass a wedding celebration, traffic signals, the Staff
    Selection Commission,
And news of deaths, one after another. My legs tremble, my
    nose
Bleeds, but I don't faint. On my left shoulder my mother
    sings
Semi-classical Bengali songs, on my right, my father
    watches TV

An action movie. And I stand with my feet planted on the
heads
Of my self-absorbed father and mother, yes, I. Who cares
nothing
For getting a job, disdains the poet's fame, doesn't want to
fret
Over love and separation, who only wants to see the world
ending at once.

God and Apples

It's absolutely true that god eats apples with his rice
Those of us who have seen the man up close know
Every morning, disguised in a lungi and shirt, he
Buys vegetables, prawns, and so on, before
Reading the newspaper with his high-powered glasses
His wife goes to work, they have no children, he
Manages to pass the afternoon and evening in sleep
He sleeps because he has to stay up every night
In the poky living room by an oilstained light…
A brass plate of rice on a three-legged table
At which god sits and eats, but not just the rice
Two or three apples turn up suddenly on his plate
It's not a big deal, happens every night, inevitably
But before you know it the number of apples rises
As the night deepens, they no longer fit on the plate,
Apples are heaped on the table, floor, everywhere.
His wife sleeps, the fridge sleeps, the TV glows blue…
He is not perturbed. One by one, patiently, he eats
The bunch of rotten apples, their pus oozing out
God eats them all by himself, staying up all night
The apples we don't eat but pass on to our maids…

Pablo and the Postman
(After watching *Il Postino*)

The postman you had befriended
Gathers dry leaves now and
Sings an unfamiliar tune to himself

I'm looking for sustenance in end-rhymes
I've bought sleep, a broken moon, wicker chairs
Wondering how long it will be to tranquillity

The lake whose shores you used to wander on
Is as dry as a stone which I've put in a ring
In the worthless hope that my luck will turn

Colour-coordinated scraps of flattery in the morning
Solitary walks in the afternoon… How will I
Write you letters in my language anymore

The city air is a bilious green, the trees, poisonous
I refer to writing as a bad habit now
Breaking old glass panes with new pebbles

Only an enchanted madman, lazy, gaunt
Gathering dry leaves all day
The postman you had befriended

Asha Naznin

Feminist poet of the 2000s from Bangladesh.

A Claim for Possession

I wish to buy you, my love
Claiming personal possession – just the way the deed of a
    house
Carries the owner's name

Didn't some shameless hussy call you to her by your
    nickname the other day?
Can my lover be a local bus who stops every time he's
    hailed?

The river saw a parade of glowworms on a night coloured
    orange with gunpowder, the beautiful bathing in the
    moon's caresses
In the moonlight the river kissed him in complete secrecy
That river is dry today, destitute. The beautiful still
    descends
At midnight, his body now held by a river in her prime
Even the mynah that flies away to perch in the bamboo
    grove hides its lover
For fear of losing him. Birds don't know how to sue, just as
    the Bengali woman cannot be happy
With the receipt of alimony from a husband who has
    forsaken her.

Before love bankrupts me I wish to buy you, so that you can
    never hit the stockmarket
To hell with all this democracy and socialism; love means
    nothing but female dictatorship, noble one
You are in my grasp alone; I would like to remind you
    again.

Any exception
Will lead to your being burnt alive, my boy; I'll surround
    your home with several hundred trucks piled with sand
Your front yard will be filled with ammunition

Hence my cordial invitation to thou, exalted one – transfer
    one hundred per cent of thy ownership to me.

I shall not shortchange you, I wish to buy you at a price of
    one billion kisses
If someone lovelier bids a higher price this evening, I swear
    by the lord
I'm ready to pay two billion too.
In cash or in instalments.
But still I must have your complete future ownership.

End notes

The translated poems 'Postmen in the Autumnal Forest', 'Not a very happy time', 'The Rain On Calcutta's Breast', and 'The Girl Named Mungri' by Shakti Chattopadhyay originally appeared in *Very Close to Pleasure, There's a Sick Cat and Other Poems*, Shakti Chattopadhyay, Seagull Books, 2017.

The translated poems 'When Will Winter Come, Suparna?', 'Tangles', and 'The Language of Giraffes' by Bhaskar Chakrabarti originally appeared in *Things That Happen and Other Poems*, Bhaskar Chakravarti, Seagull Books, 2016.

The translated poems 'For Neera, Unexpectedly', 'Exile',

'Got The Blues', and 'No One Kept Their Word' by Sunil Gangopadhyay originally appeared in *You are Neera*, Sunil Gangopadhyay, Harper-Collins India, 2014.

The translator is grateful to all the poets whose works appear in this anthology.

Sanchit Art is an Indian art gallery selling modern and contemporary artworks of various Indian master artists. It also aims to bridge the gap between artists working in India and abroad by establishing a platform to show contemporary European art in India while reciprocating the same with curated shows of contemporary Indian art abroad. The gallery, at New Delhi, is equipped with modern facilities for display and appreciation of conventional as well as new age mediums. This is a gallery with a difference, aimed primarily at offering a panoramic review of modern & contemporary Indian art.

Born 1954 in Kolkata, **Shipra Bhattacharya** is a B.Sc. graduate, who later studied Fine Art at the College of Visual Arts, Kolkata. Ever since her first solo show in Kolkata in 1981, she has made her presence felt on the country's thriving art scene with numerous solo and group shows all over India and at London and in New York. Her work adorns various public, corporate and private collections. She lives in Kolkata and works from her studio at home.

Her canvases often revolve around a feminine figure entrapped within and encasing her dream world submerged in intricate renderings. While the female figure forms a central part of her work, it is more the inner consciousness of these women that the artist draws on, using bold yet soft colours and smooth brushwork.